help

ROYCE MURCHERSON, PH.D

THE GUIDE TO
PERSUASIVE
BUSINESS WRITING

A NEW MODEL THAT GETS RESULTS

SECOND EDITION

Kendall Hunt
publishing company

Cover image © Shutterstock, Inc.; p315, © AF studio/Shutterstock.com; p318(t), © Constantin Stanciu/Shutterstock.com; p318(c), © photo5963_shutter/Shutterstock.com; p318(b), © Igor Petrov/Shutterstock.com

Kendall Hunt
publishing company

www.kendallhunt.com
Send all inquiries to:
4050 Westmark Drive
Dubuque, IA 52004-1840

CONTENTS

SECTION 3 – THE BUSINESS OF PERSUASION
the toulmin model and persuasive business writing

SECTION 4 – WHAT HAPPENED TO THE MEMO?
....is it email or what?

SECTION 5 – CLOSING THE DEAL
writing persuasive letters

SECTION 6 – HIRED!
how to write persuasive job application letters and resumes

SECTION 7 – STATUS PLEASE!
short informal reports in the workplace

SECTION 8 – WHY IS IT IMPORTANT? CONVINCE ME ALREADY!
proposals and the executive summary

SECTION 9 – WORKING TO WIN!
strategies you should know

WHY THIS BOOK IS A KEEPER
A message from the author

Why is this book a keeper? I wrote it with one purpose in mind—you. My objective is to help you become a competent persuasive writer. What might this get you? What most of us want: to be successful. You will be busy. You will need to make a good impression quickly. Because of this, I have been careful to include many examples of documents you will be likely to create at some time in your career. As far as explanations of how to write these documents, I have tried to keep it 'short and sweet,' that is, give you the most important information in the most concise manner.

Remember, on the first day of the job, every day on the job, you will be creating your own narrative, writing your story, creating an image. And the quality of your story will depend on how you communicate it. Good persuasive writing will have much to do with this.

The whole idea of writing persuasive business documents is not new. Your bosses or supervisors will need to be persuaded to accept your good ideas, solutions, and improvements. A great personality, sports statistics, and really interesting 'water cooler' talk is not a guarantee for a bright future. Communication in the form of clear, effective writing that sells your 'intellect' is the key.

So what makes this guide different? How is it going to help you other than providing examples of different types of business documents? This guide is a new approach to business writing that uses a common sense model you can learn and use easily. So yes, this model is new to persuasive business writing, but it is also based on an old model of argumentation referred to as the Toulmin Model of Argumentation and is still taught in college and university classrooms.

I have borrowed the ideas of Stephen Toulmin from his book, The Uses of Argument, 1958. In it, he argues logic as a means to rational argument. It is a scholarly difficult read that is based more on the 'science' and 'theory' of argument than the common sense use of its practices. This is what I have attempted to do in this book, turn the theoretical into practical to help you get ahead today.

What I attempt to do in this guide is to communicate Toulmin's explanation of the pattern of argument in an easy-to-read, easy-to-understand way. The originality of this book lies in the way I apply his model to business writing. It is a user-friendly method for writing persuasive documents that get results. Keep it in your desk, in your backpack, or your locker. Just keep it and learn from it.

—Royce Murcherson, Ph. D.

THE GOOD, THE BAD, AND THE UN-EASY

ETHICAL BEHAVIOR IN THE WORKPLACE

Remember when you were a kid? When it came to what was good and what was bad, it was pretty clear. When you were good, there was ice cream in your future. When you were bad, it was off to the time out corner. It was never a case of either/or. Nowadays you're all grown up. You've figured out that the rules can be bent at times for one reason or the other. And sometimes you've probably indulged because it was pretty harmless. Afterward, you may have felt a little uneasy about it, but hey, no laws were broken, right? It's that feeling of uneasiness when you're not sure that you've made the right decision that is important.

Certain voices will explain ethical behavior in the workplace as a list of things 'not to do.' Things like, *never plagiarize*. You remember this from freshman composition. Then there's hiding information, exaggerating claims, copyright infringement, crossing cultural boundaries, and conflicts of interest.

This is all well and good if you've already been working in a business environment and you have some sense of behavior based on experience. In other words, you've had a few bumps along the way when making choices, realized that every choice has its consequences and in turn managed them whether good or bad.

1

WHAT DO YOU KNOW ABOUT ETHICS?

But's let's assume you've not made it this far in the world of business. Let's assume you never really gave ethics a second thought when it comes to being on a job. Let's assume you never took a philosophy of ethics course too. Don't worry, you're okay. But first let's get to some basic questions in simple language.

What is it, what does it really mean?

When and why did it get to be an issue in the workplace?

Why do I need to know anything about it?

What's the value of it?

Can I get damaged if I don't know anything about ethics?

All of these questions can be answered with two words, PROFESSIONAL SUCCESS.

Do you want to be happy? Do you want to be successful?

Success = Happiness = Success.

Aren't these your main goals in life, to be happy and to be successful? Of course, but there are many ways to get to the happiness professional success can give. But we need to understand where this natural inclination comes from and how it could harm us if we do not go about getting it in an ethical way.

WHAT'S HAPPINESS GOT TO DO WITH IT?

It's Human Nature. A philosopher by the name of John Stuart Mill understood that people want to be as happy as possible. He wrapped up his theories about this in a work called *Utilitarianism* published in 1861. *According to the Greatest Happiness Principle...the ultimate end...is an existence exempt as far as possible from pain, and as rich as possible in enjoyments.*

Ultimately, we as humans want to be happy, our happiness can be tied to many things. In this case, let's focus on professional success and the next obvious question. How is ethical behavior tied to professional success?

WHAT DOES ETHICAL BEHAVIOR MEAN?

First, let's define it. Ethics is a set of principles that govern an individual or group's behavior. These principles can come down to beliefs such as treating others as you would want to be treated. These principles can also come down to intuition, some inner feeling or moral compass that helps you decide what is right and what is wrong. This is what it comes down too…this question…what is the right thing to do?

A sense of justice, individual rights, and understanding the consequences of your actions has much to do with your sense of right and wrong. These concepts are important and should certainly be included in your world view. But for the purposes of this section, I'll try to keep it as simple as possible and relate it to 'real world situations' in the office, real questions that you will need to ask yourself when making 'choices.'

Your choices will govern your behavior. Your behavior can in turn create an image of you that can either be considered ethical or unethical. For morality's sake, I would hope that you choose ethical over unethical because there can be an effective argument framed on both sides. This is the difficult part.

WHAT PRICE ARE YOU WILLING TO PAY FOR SUCCESS?

You will find yourself having to make choices when it comes to how you work with others and in what fashion you fulfill your duties and responsibilities. These ethical choices will come down to understanding the real difference between what is right and what is wrong but it's not that simple. Our culture is dramatically affected by changing values and beliefs on so many levels to the extent that what is right and what is wrong can be relative. Figuring out the correct answer could depend on situations and circumstance. What can be considered wrong in one situation could be considered right in another.

> **For Example:** John is the only wage earner in his family. He was laid off and has not been able to find a job in three months. Unemployment insurance and his family savings cover the rent, utilities, and gas, and food. The savings account is almost gone. He has been cutting corners to make it last which has come down to his family eating one meal a day. John goes to the grocery store and is trying to buy the most with the money he has. Meat is a luxury. He sees a pork tenderloin that he cannot afford. John adds it to his cart, heads to the most obscure corner he can find and hides the tenderloin in his backpack. He has just committed theft.

The Big Question:

Was this the right thing to do or the wrong thing to do?

What's The Answer?

The answer is completely relative. It will depend on an individual's unique understanding of 'right' and wrong' and how it fits into real world events that are never written the same, never the same circumstances and situations. So there is no one, definitive, correct answer. You can make an argument on both sides. You can argue that John did the right thing for his family's sake by giving them something special, something to put a smile on their faces, to feed them. You can also argue that he did the wrong thing by committing theft. Meat is not an absolute necessity to prevent starvation. You are now squarely in the middle of an ethical dilemma.

ETHICAL DILEMMAS IN THE WORKPLACE

Image © Maharani, 2013. Used under license from Shutterstock, Inc.

Figure: 1.1   Here's a picture of a weasel. Weasels are by definition cunning and devious.

You may find yourself in a location where *situation and circumstance* can come into play and affect how you understand the difference between right behavior and wrong behavior. In the example, John more than likely feels he is doing the right thing for his family. You as an observer may see it as theft pure and simple, or you may see it as the wrong thing but with unique circumstances that turns 'wrong' into '*not so wrong*' or what we like to refer to as an exception to the rule.

This is the grey zone between 'right' and 'wrong', that is, a place in which a person has the opportunity to circumvent definitions of right behavior and wrong behavior. In other words, the meanings may change due to relevance. You may begin to think how you can **go around or avoid by artful maneuvering**. Try not to find yourself in a position where you must circumvent what you understand as 'right behavior.' **Don't be a Weasel**.

GUIDELINES: Avoid 'Weaseling-Out'

- Don't be sneaky in your dealings, achieving success by underhanded methods.
- Don't be cunning in order to advance selfish interests or hurt others.
- Don't be evasive in your communication with others. Be straightforward. Do not be intentionally vague or ambiguous.
- Don't be deceptive in your actions, misleading deliberately.
- Don't be cowardly. Display confidence. Try to set a good example when dealing with tough issues.
- Don't evade responsibility. Do not back out of commitments. cultivate cooperative behavior that benefits the group.

THE 'GREY ZONE'

The big challenge you will face in workplace ethics is learning how to live in the 'grey zone.' Here comes that feeling of un-easiness again. You'll generally feel it when you know that the right thing to do is what you shouldn't do, the wrong thing to do is not an option, and the in-between is not very comfortable either.

In director, Sidney Lumet's crime drama, *Night Falls on Manhattan* (1996), there is a closing scene where the district attorney is addressing a group of newly hired assistant district attorneys. He is giving them some cautionary advice on their future work environment.

> He tells them, *"I found myself in a position where breaking the law was more just than upholding the law and upholding the law killed a man...I don't have to prepare you for a job where circumstances are black and white...you're gonna spend most of your time in the grey areas and I guarantee you're gonna come face to face with who you really are."*

You will more than likely find yourself there most of the time as well. And in turn, you will ultimately figure out the kind of person you are. So ask yourself now. What kind of person do I want to be?

All of your decisions and choices may not be simple and straightforward, this way or that way without any space in-between. You will need to understand that when it comes to right behavior and wrong behavior in the workplace, situation and circumstance may give you the option of stepping into the 'grey zone'. You will need to remember that the 'grey zone' is a place that can at times be used to justify doing the 'wrong thing' for what you believe are right reasons. When you clearly understand how this zone can be used to interpret the difference between right and wrong behavior, remember your basic understanding of right and wrong, perhaps you will be able to make the right choice.

Question: What can help me make ethical decisions in the grey zone?

Answer: Understand the 'me condition'

THE ME-CONDITION

In plain language, how does our world influence our decisions when it comes to 'right behavior' and 'wrong behavior'? It all comes down to *ego*. As a psychological term, ego is *you, your sense of self, you the individual, or the conscious you*. Sometimes it means an exaggerated sense of self-importance which brings us to this well known expression: *'It's not about you'* or *'it's not about me.'*

I like to call this the *'me-condition,'* that place or time in which an individual will base all of their decisions and choices on personal interests. Kurt Baier explains it in his article, *Egoism*.

> He states, *"...egoism involves putting one's own good, interest, and concern above that of others."* He continues by explaining egoists as people *"... whose motivated behavior...protects and promotes their own welfare, well-being, best interest, happiness...or greater good either because they are indifferent about that of others or because they care more about their own..."*

Figure: 1.2   Relationship Equation for Egoism

So what's wrong with keeping your own self-interest above everything else? You want to be a success right? You want the American Dream right? Remember the price, what price are you willing to pay? Keeping self-interest in mind can be a good thing in many ways. It can also lead to behavior that runs contrary to other people's best interest. You may find yourself in the grey where situation and circumstance will influence your choices in either a negative or positive way. It's hard not to think of your own best interest first. How do we manage the *me-condition* in the grey zone?

Here's an example from real life that can illustrate how good intentions result in self-interest:

> In 2012, Hurricane Sandy devastated important areas of the northeast coast. The state of New Jersey was hit particularly hard. A democratic President and a republican governor have both requested federal aid to help rebuild the New Jersey coastline. Congress has the power to appropriate 60 billion dollars in aid. This hurricane relief is attached to a bill that will cut taxes on middle income Americans and raise taxes on the wealthiest Americans to help pay down the national debt without hurting the economically hard hit middle class. Republicans in the Congress are opposed to this bill because they oppose any increases in taxes, even the top 1 percent of Americans or those that make over 400,000 dollars per year. If Republicans vote against the tax bill, they will have to vote against hurricane relief. To vote for hurricane relief, the Republicans would have to vote for the tax bill which would increase taxes on the top 1 percent of Americans. The Republican Speaker of the House removed the hurricane relief item and denied any vote to appropriate 60 billion dollars to rebuild the New Jersey coastline.

Because the Republican Congress was so committed to not raising taxes on the very wealthy, they stripped the hurricane relief from the bill in order to avoid having to vote for a tax increase. The residents and businesses of the New Jersey shore were denied funds based on political interests. The Republican Congress failed to anticipate the public outrage when it chose to place political ideology above morality and interest for others.

MAKING ETHICAL DECISIONS IN THE GREY ZONE

It can be very difficult to make ethical decisions in the grey zone where situation and circumstance come into play, and even harder when the *me condition* kicks in. The diagram below can serve as a standard by which to make ethical decisions. When confronted with such a decision, take the time to ask yourself the following three questions, and then make your decision based on your response to each.

| How will I benefit? |
| How could my benefit hurt or help others? |
| What kind of person do I want to be? |

Figure: 1.3 Criteria for Making Ethical Decisions

The Golden Rule in Workplace Ethics: Temper self-interest and cultivate cooperative behavior that benefits the group.

There are many sources that detail legal guidelines, copyright laws, liability law, reporting ethical abuses, and fair and honest communication. It's a lot to read and remember if you can locate them. Most companies will have a code of ethics or corporate conduct. Be sure to inquire with the human resources department, read it, understand it and follow through. Employment can be terminated if there are violations of conduct. But for now, how can we keep it simple and straightforward? It all comes down to a few simple common sense questions.

WORKPLACE GUIDELINES for Ethical Behavior

Should I share?

- Yes.
- Never withhold information from supervisors and colleagues that will help or protect.
- Never suppress knowledge that can affect or influence events in negative or positive ways.

Should I be trustworthy?

- Yes.
- Trust is a wonderful thing. You need to be able to count on your colleagues and supervisors to be your 'back up.' Foster trustworthy relationships by having a 'teamwork' attitude.

Should I take responsibility?

- Yes.
- Make sure you understand your responsibilities as an employee.
- Always take responsibility for your actions, good or bad.
- Never shirk responsibility by passing it off to others.
- Never back away from responsibility if you are asked to perform additional tasks.

Should I be professional?

- Yes.
- Always be on time to work. Manage your lunch breaks.
- Never engage in idle office gossip that will hurt or demean your colleagues.
- Never be loud or coercive in your dealings with colleagues and supervisors. Keep a civil and congenial tone.
- Be open to change and maintain a positive attitude.

Should I show commitment?

- Yes.
- Be committed to doing the best job possible.
- Invest time in perfecting or gaining new skills.
- Never be afraid to go the extra mile and spend more time in the office.
- Always look for opportunities to improve your work process.

Should I lie? –

- Absolutely not.
- Never falsify data or misrepresent events.
- Sustain honest communication with colleagues, supervisors, and managers.

Should I steal?

- Absolutely not.
- Understand how plagiarism works, don't do it. Never appropriate information that is not your own without citing the source or giving credit to the original author.
- Understand copyright laws such as the 'fair use' policy. Do not infringe on copyrights.
- Do not leak proprietary information from your company: financial records, plans, product specifications etc.

Should I cheat?

- Absolutely not.
- Never exaggerate claims of performance, events, and results.
- Understand 'conflicts of interest.'

CORPORATE CODES OF CONDUCT

Most corporations will encourage a culture that is ethical. They will vary in degree. Some will ask that a prospective employee signs a code of conduct and tie his or her employment to it should any infractions occur. The codes will vary. They will usually ask employees to accept responsibility in making decisions. They will ask employees to avoid conflicts of interest. They decry any form of discrimination such as: racial, ethnic, age, gender, disability. It is also not unusual for corporations to include a statement that addresses protection of the company's intellectual property. They can encourage a safe workplace where employees must avoid injuring others and their property. Bottom line, codes of legal and ethical conduct will vary per company. Some companies will be weak, some companies will be strong. It's a good idea to keep this in mind when you apply for employment.

Exercises:

1. You are a member of a four person paralegal team in the law firm of Wresting and Wresting. It is what your dad use to call a 'good ole boys club.' Your team leader is a woman. You have been with the firm four months. Your leader has always stressed the 'sharing of information.' She has always encouraged you to ask questions, and be inquisitive when it comes to the law. Your team works in the same open space, each desk is next to the other with very little privacy. It is lunch time; everyone on the team is out of the office. You pass by your team leader's desk and notice a pile of mail in her inbox. You see a brief on top that details a big upcoming case. You would like to know the details so that you can talk about the law with the partners in the break room rather than about football. Is it ethical to open the brief and read the contents given the fact your team leader has encouraged you to be inquisitive?
2. You are applying for a job as an import manager. The requirements of the job include a proficiency in three basic types of office software. You are familiar with two of them. Even though you know nothing about the third, spreadsheet, you plan to learn it on the

job if you get hired. You will write your cover letter so that it does not specifically mention each type of software. Is it ethical to be vague? Is it ethical to apply for the job in the first place knowing you do not meet all of the requirements?

Image © blinkblink, 2013. Used under license from Shutterstock, Inc.

OFF-FICE-SPEAK

KEEPING THE 'RIGHT' TONE IN BUSINESS WRITING

OVERVIEW

Tone can be a tricky concept to master because it's difficult to understand. Not understanding how powerful tone can be can you into some uncomfortable situations. It can cause you to be misunderstood by others. For example, if you were rushing through an email message somewhat angry that you were behind in your work, it can come across to your audience as if you were angry at them when in fact you were angry at yourself. It is very easy to write your mood into a message and unintentionally offend others.

All academic and professional writing should maintain a formal tone throughout the work. That's sort of hard. Why? Because we pretty much live in an online environment which is largely informal. We go about our daily lives speaking, texting, tweeting in everyday language. So naturally when you begin to write, your brain is going to transfer that same informality to your paper because it is the only thing it knows out of habit.

Having success in the palm of our hands is what we all want, but to get there nothing needs to be taken for granted, namely, proper business communication. Proper speaking and writing is the key to success. In this online world, work colleagues and bosses will only know you through what and how you write: email, proposals, instant messaging. Words and how you use them become your face. You are creating an image that may have little to do with the real flesh and blood you and everything to do with your style of writing. If you write on the whacky side of things, then you may be perceived as whacky. If you indulge in urban slang excessively, then you may be perceived as such.

Some of your colleagues will never have the privilege of meeting you face to face and building a traditional relationship. They will have to rely on your messaging. So make your messaging worth of 'who you truly are' and 'how you wish to be known'.

A DEEPER DISCUSSION OF TONE

Tone in Electronic Communication

With electronic communication in the business world nowadays, you rarely have to face the person on the other end so it becomes easy to hide behind a wall of transactions like "reply and delete," "follow-up, clean up, and forward." Do not think of email as a solid wall that protects you from outside forces. It's exactly the opposite, it opens you up to outside forces. Your writing and the tone you create in your messages can make you an open book; that is, open to other people's interpretations of you. Try not to let this happen.

You will send many messages in the workplace. Typically, most of them will be in the form of email and instant messaging. But depending on your job, you may also be tasked with more formal writing such as letters, memos, and progress reports to name a few.

Just as the singing contestants in the NBC series, *The Voice*, work to create the most beautiful tone and win the contest, you must also work to create the most appropriate tone in your business writing. How? By understanding the origin of tone, and understanding what it takes to ensure your tone is always appropriate. Because the concept of tone is challenging and requires explanation and exercises, let's confine our discussion to two basic questions and some solid advice.

Question # 1: What is tone?

- Tone is Attitude. And attitude is a state of mind that can be passed on in our words.

Question #2: How do you know when your tone is appropriate?

- Your tone is appropriate when you take the "mood out of the message."

Solid Advice:

Understand Emotional Mine Fields To keep the mood out of the message, know how to navigate the emotional mine fields. It's good to have a happy and upbeat attitude, but what about the times when you are not particularly happy and upbeat? These are the times when you must work to keep your mood out of your message. Think about sleepless nights, car troubles, family matters, and workload deadlines. These can drive the tone of your message and can wreak havoc in business communication. On the flip side, think about successes. Don't let them go to your head. Remember, you are a member of the team and must treat your colleagues with respect. It can be easy to slip into the, "I'm the king of the world" attitude (*Titanic*, Twentieth Century Fox, 1997).

Avoid Booby Traps in the Mine Fields As you make your way through the mine fields, don't be caught off guard and let your emotions lead you into the trap of…

- **Being Contentious** – Do not use combative, bombastic language that suggests you are the conqueror and your colleagues are the conquered. Remember, cultivating teamwork means success for all.
- **Being Arrogant** – Do not use high-flying over-bloated language that would suggest you're the smartest in the room. Remember, it's possible you have a lot to learn from your teammates.
- **Being Bossy** – Do not use pretentious and domineering language as if you have been given the "alpha" role. Remember, this decision likely rests with others.

Attitude

Tone is Attitude. And attitude is a state of mind that can be passed on in our words. Think of your writing as if it could have its own attitude. And just as people around us can tell what mood we are in from the attitude we project, the people to whom we write can also tell. Depending on mood or occasion, the attitude in our writing can change from formal to informal, semi formal to funny, positive to negative, arrogant to humble. When we understand how words can communicate attitude or mood, we can select the right ones to convey the message we wish.

Do Not Write Like This! What's tone? I'll tell you what it is. It's something that's a career maker and a career breaker. Tone can make a deal or tank a deal. Tone can mess up an employment application. Tone can sink a business proposal that should a landed you a raise in salary, or could a got you a bigger office.

OMG, tone is the whatever, the what-if, the hook-up, the bomb. It'll get you in the end if you don't watch out. I'm speaking the truth. Know what I'm sayin?

Everything you just read was the worst possible way to communicate with anyone in the business world. But it's the best possible way to talk to your friends because it's what they expect you to sound like.

Here's another version of what you just read. None of your friends would expect you to **talk** like this...but your boss would expect you to...

Write like this You ask the question, what is tone? Tone is an extremely important factor to consider when communicating at work. It can make your career or break your career. Important deals may fall through if the tone is inappropriate. Employment applications and business proposals can also suffer. Tone is undoubtedly the most underemphasized transaction in corporate communication. Understanding it will save your professional life. This is a simple truth.

The first paragraph describing tone is informal, the one above is formal. See the difference? It should be fairly obvious. Bottom line, there are different types of tone, different attitudes. I am writing this section in an informal tone because we are having a conversation of sorts. I am being conversational. I want to identify with you and speak in a language that's familiar. When people talk to each other in an everyday situation, they are not speaking formally. But when we write for business, it should be formal.

ATTITUDE ADJUSTMENT

Just as we can adjust our attitude from good to bad to indifferent, we can adjust the tone in our writing from formal to semiformal, to informal.

Types of Tone

- formal
- semi-formal
- informal

Some Examples of Tone

Excerpted from "Cat People vs. Dog People" by Laura Miller

Formal Tone

Of the questions that perplex humanity, some are eternal. What is the meaning of Life? Do we have a spiritual essence that survives our material existence?...Why does "Sex and the City' have a reputation for featuring fabulous clothes when most of the time poor Sarah Jessica parker is dressed up like an organ grinder's monkey? Still others are mundane, yet persistent…Which is better, Mac or PC?....Who are more annoying, cat people or dog people?....

Semi-formal Tone

There are many questions that confuse humanity and some are even eternal. How about the meaning of life? What about spirituality? Do we survive past our human bodies? Why do people think that the television program, "Sex and the City" is all about fashion when the lead actress dresses bad? Whatever the reason, these questions aren't going away. For instance, 'which is better, Mac or PC?'…or 'Who are more annoying, cat people or dog people?'…..

Informal Tone

There are a lotta questions people ask over and over again. Like, what's the meaning of life? Or the craziest one, is reincarnation real or bogus? And the stupidest one about that television program, *Sex and the City*. Why does Carrie wear clothes that are not all that when the show wants us to believe that the fashion is so on top of it? Who cares really, like whether cat people are weirder than dog people?

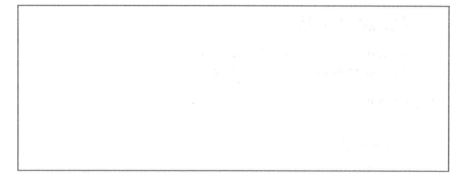

Practice Drill: What are the basic differences between the formal, semi-formal, and informal versions above? Compare each sentence. Look at the choice of words. Are they basically saying the same thing with more or less words? Are the words friendlier, less like a research article? Make some notes below and check your response against the answer key to see how you do. See the answer key at the end of this section.

Business writing should be formal or semi-formal in most occasions. This means it should be dispassionate or devoid of emotion. Your reader should never be able to pick up on things like anger, sarcasm, frustration, or even overt happiness. Don't be too 'dark' or negative. Remember, you'll be speaking to your boss and your colleagues. Bottom line, your paycheck may depend on it.

Keep the Mood Out of the Message

People who get accused of being 'mean' or 'nasty' in email are usually the ones who do not have a clue. Yes, this is a very informal way to put it, but let's be real. Earlier, I wrote about how our mood can influence our attitude and how our attitude can affect the tone of our writing. This is a simple rule, best to remember it.

We all have bad days, good days, and in-between days. We have days when we haven't had enough sleep the night before. We have days when everything is going great away from work, so why go to work? It's the mood we find ourselves in that can change the course of things during a work day when it comes to the way we communicate, particularly in our writing.

When we put words on paper, they are there, they are read, and they live in the minds of the reader. In short, they are hard to 'take back' for better or worst. This is why you must be particularly diligent when it comes to containing your mood in your writing, good or bad.

Why is it Important to Keep the Mood out of the Message?

- **Know that your mood can be caused by a single emotional response** or a conglomerate of responses. Emotional responses include such things as anger, sadness, indifference, arrogance, and sarcasm. If you need to take some time, take the time and write when you are feeling calm, clear, and objective.
- **Know that your readers may misunderstand** and think your emotional response is their fault, or that you are directing your anger at them when in fact you are angry with yourself.
- **Know that electronic messages are practically eternal** in cyberspace. They may never be fully deleted either on the server or in the minds of your colleagues.
- **Know that words have consequences.** What you think is acceptable or funny may be offensive to others. Do not use slang or overly familiar language. Do not use text-speak. Do not use expletives of any kind. Use Standard English and practice good grammar and spelling. Stay away from humor.

Contentious Email

Here's the thing about email or any electronic writing. It's easier to be brave when you do not have to face the person involved. Plainly put, it's easy to hide behind an email. Do not think of email as some protective covering. You will either have to face the person eventually, or you may do great damage to your reputation. There will always be things you want to say but cannot. It takes much more energy to keep words to yourself rather than putting them on paper. So think control. The worst offender is the 'contentious email.' Here are two examples of inappropriate email messages questioning grades.

Examples:

Version 1 – Angry and Combative.
Wow.. Really.. I worked my ass off to keep up with this course.. A reminder that it would close at noon would have been nice.. I took off work just to study for the final.. Thanks for nothing.... ... So much for striving to do your best and having support of your teachers... Vey disappointed.....

Version 2 – Angry and Emotional.
I had registered for British literature but I changed and thought I should learn something new "American literature," so if I did not do it right, I should not be accused of cheating with my own work. I am glad I am furthering my education, and at this level with your help I thought it would lead to my dreams coming true but I see that instead my dreams are being shut.

Revisions:

Version 1 –
Professor,
I am very sorry that I did not take my final exam. I misunderstood the closing date announcement. Please consider the fact that I took off work to study for the final. I hoped to make a better than average grade in your class. I need your support. Would you be willing to re open the course and let me take the final?

Version 2 –
Professor,
I believe there may be some mistake with regard to my assignment. I did not cut and paste another author's work. May I schedule an office appointment to discuss this? When I registered for this course, I chose American Literature rather than British Literature so that I could learn something new. I am glad to be furthering my education, but I need to get past this 'cheating' issue to realize my dreams.

Further Examples: Inner Office Email

Version 1. Fine, there is a memo—a plan. It is all disjointed; there is no real focus or consistency. I've made this point before and nobody responded. Given this, can you explain why I should buy into this? This is about consistency. So, we can go round and round on email or we can have a meeting. I don't think anything concrete can be done until this takes place.

Revison:

Version 1. Thanks to Dan who worked on the memo. It was a good plan but perhaps deserves some adjustments. We might consider focusing on two outcomes rather than four. This would provide more consistency. Earlier, I suggested this but it did not meet with much enthusiasm. Now, time is of the essence. Trying to solve this issue via email will not serve us well. Let's meet in person.

GUIDELINES for a formal tone:

- Remember that errors in tone can be whole sentences, paragraphs, phrases, and single words that break the rules.
- Do not write your mood into the message. Stay objective and sterile. Overt emotion is not a good thing. Remember, it is not about YOU.
- Use first person sparingly. It is very informal. 1st person is when you use personal pronouns like *I, me, and mine, our.*
- Try to use 3rd person. 3rd person is less informal. 3rd person is when you use pronouns like they, them, he, she, oneself. As in the first guideline, keep yourself out of the dialogue as much as possible. Keep it objective.

- Avoid slang: Do not use words and phrases like 'dawg'-'hook-up'-whatever - 'that's so harsh', shake down, power trip, step off.
- Avoid relaxed language and colloquialisms: gonna, wanna, shoulda, coulda, got, ya'll, know what I mean? I'm just sayin, keep it real.
- Avoid contractions like don't, won't, and can't. Instead, use words like *do not, cannot,* and *will not.*
- Avoid the funny stuff: Humor only works when you are good at it, that is, a professional or natural comedian. The trap is what may be funny to you could be offensive to others.

Section 1 Recap:

Stay objective and relatively sterile in your writing. This does not mean academic and professional writing has to be boring. It can have some life in it, but it must still strike an objective sober tone. It should never read or sound as if you are speaking to a friend on the sofa. So read your paper out loud to someone and ask them to judge the difference between your writing and your everyday speaking. Then revise if necessary.

Keeping a formal tone in your writing puts you in the right direction towards success. If you are worried that your readers may never know the fun loving laid back you, don't worry about it. If they are impressed by your smarts which is what your writing will convey, they will eventually meet the real you outside cyberspace. Then you can bring both your sides together, the everyday you and the serious thoughtful professional. It's difficult to have it both ways in this competitive job market, so play it safe. If you play it fast and loose, the whole idea of straight to the top could end of being any which way but right.

Complete the exercises at the end of this section. Answer keys will follow the exercises.

Exercise #1:

The following letter is an inquiry for employment. Review the guidelines for tone and locate the errors in tone or grammar by underlining or circling. You may check your answers against the answer key.

Sara Costanza, Personnel Director
Liberty International, Inc.
Lansdowne, PA 24153

Dear Ms. Costanza:

Please consider my application for a entry level management position at your Lake Geneva shipping line as advertised on November 1 thru Career-Builder's. I'll graduate college December 2012 from Rice University with a B.A. in International Business. I know my experience is pretty close to what companies might want given I'm about to graduate and haven't had much direct experience. My dream job is to work as a logistic manager for a major international container shipping line and what your seeking falls in line to what I'm pursuing.

As you can see from my enclosed resume, I landed and intern position thru APL lines the Summer of 2008 where I worked in export documentation and created international bills of lading for global accounts. I learned all about shipping lanes, how goods are rated for shipping cost, insurance, arrival times, and even restrictions on goods going to certain countries. During the previous Summer, I worked at the same shipping line as a dock worker loading shipping containers.

Just wearing a tie or nice trousers looks good but it's also good to be able to say I loaded the containers. I've gotten my hands dirty learning from the bottom up. I am well aware of the expectations for this position and hope my Summer intern and related skills will show you my passion for this industry.

I bring relevant experience to the table so you won't have to worry about training me if hired. I'm disciplined, energetic, and a quick learner. I confident I will be an asset to the team.

If my background meets your needs, please call anytime after 11a.m. to (972)-777-9311 or email me at jturner2829@yahoo.com.

Sincerely,

Bill Connelly

Exercise #2:

Read both paragraphs. Decide which one is informal. Circle it and underline all of the informal words and phrases. You can check your answers in the answer key section.

   A. The world of business writing is often considered sterile. It is an objective universe that does not consider emotional phrasing, overly negative commentary or undue sentiments of kindness. Interlopers consider business writing devoid of personality while the Inhabitants of this world see it as grammatically responsible and conservative in approach.

   B. I think business writing is whack. It's got no life man, no feelings. I don't wanna know what universes these people live it that like it so much. I just think anyone who likes it must not have much of a personality. I mean, I wouldn't friend them on my Facebook page because I couldn't understand what they're saying in the first place. It'd be like friending a Republican, hee hee.

Exercise #3:

The statements below would sound like a foreign language in any typical business communication. Translate them by rewriting each in a more formal tone. You may check your answers in the answer key section.

   1. I wanna attend the meeting this afternoon.
   2. If the orders don't ship today, we'll definitely loose money, know what I'm sayin?
   3. Couldn't of gone to the employee lunch if I wanted too. Had too much work.
   4. You better step off and get back to your cubicle and finish your work.
   5. Things shoulda gone better if we had been better prepared.
   6. That third quarter report is so not there this year.
   7. His administrative assistant is so dizzy.
   8. Don't bet bent outta shape if you don't get the raise you wanted.
   9. Last year's Christmas bonuses were the bomb.
   10. He ditched the meeting and went site seeing instead.
   11. Most of the orders from Europe are very strong and budget projections are off the hook.

12. When the seminar began, we were distracted. The presenter's dress had way too much bling going on.

13. John stopped worrying about his supervisor busting him cause he was six feet under.

14. All of the company's management directors want total success but none are prepared to do the heavy lifting.

15. Getting the progress report corrected before the meeting began was a crapshoot.

16. Company profits at the end of the quarter were a wash no matter how they try to spin it.

17. Glenn Baxter's entire proposal for new business was just smoke and mirrors.

Exercise #4:

Review the 'Guidelines for a Formal Tone.' Then circle or underline all of the informal words and phrases in the letter below addressed to Mr. John Adams at Simmons Automotive. When you are finished, check your answers against the answer key.

October 15, 2012

Mr. John Adams, General Manager
Simmons Automotive
1245 Larsen Blvd
Anderson, MO 63501

Dear Mr. Adams:

We wanna continue to be your customers no matter what. It's been 15 years, maybe more, but who's counting, right? Your company recommended we have a 30,000 mile service on our SUV. Since the service, our vehicle is consistently having trouble starting. Perhaps we should have tried another service, but since you've been around the town so long, we thought we'd come back to you, know what I mean? Anyway, whatever. So getting on with it.

We received a notice from your company to bring our SUV in for service. We did so and were charged $600.00 dollars. Upon signing for the service, I was made aware of your company guarantee that customer satisfaction was the bottom line. It explained your optimum service policy. It went like this. Any customer dissatisfaction would be addressed with a full refund. When I keyed in on this, I thought it was off the hook! But now, I am very disappointed because your customer service person told me to hit the road in so many words. She was pretty dizzy if you know what I mean.

I think you will agree that we have a problem. We were able to secure legal representation and have since taken our SUV to another automotive service. It has been determined that the fuel injection service was not performed and the spark plugs were not replaced. This would account for the failure of our vehicle to start on multiple occasions.

Look buddy, you'll be hearing from our legal peeps. They know what's what when it comes down to handling stuff this messed up. I would like you to authorize another service as soon as possible, or grant a full refund.

Ronald Cantoni

NOTES

ANSWER KEYS

Exercise #1 – Answer Key

Sara Costanza, Personnel Director
Liberty International, Inc.
Lansdowne, PA 24153

Dear Ms. Costanza:

Please consider my application for a entry level management position at your Lake Geneva shipping line as advertised on November 1 thru Career-Builder's. I'll graduate college December 2012 from Rice University with a B.A. in International Business. I know my experience is pretty close to what companies might want given I'm about to graduate and haven't had much direct experience. My dream job is to work as a logistic manager for a major international container shipping line and what your seeking falls in line to what I'm pursuing.

As you can see from my enclosed resume, I landed and intern position thru APL lines the Summer of 2008 where I worked in export documentation and created international bills of lading for global accounts. I learned all about shipping lanes, how goods are rated for shipping cost, insurance, arrival times, and even restrictions on goods going to certain countries. During the previous Summer, I worked at the same shipping line as a dock worker loading shipping containers.

Just wearing a tie or nice trousers looks good but it's also good to be able to say I loaded the containers. I've gotten my hands dirty learning from the bottom up. I am well aware of the expectations for this position and hope my summer intern and related skills will show you my passion for this industry.

I bring relevant experience to the table so you won't have to worry about training me if hired. I'm disciplined, energetic, and a quick learner. I confident I will be an asset to the team.

If my background meets your needs, please call anytime after 11a.m. to (972)-777-9311 or email me at jturner2829@yahoo.com.

Sincerely,

Bill Connelly

Exercise #2 – Answer Key

B. <u>I think</u> business writing is <u>whack</u>. <u>It's got no life man, no feel-ings</u>. <u>I don't wanna</u> know what universes these people live it that like it so much. <u>I just</u> think anyone who likes it must not have much of a personality. <u>I mean, I wouldn't</u> friend them on my Facebook page because I <u>couldn't</u> understand what <u>they're</u> saying in the first place. <u>It'd be like friending a Republican, hee hee</u>.

Exercise #3 - Answer Key

1. I wanna attend the meeting this afternoon.

   I wish to attend the meeting this afternoon.

2. If the orders don't ship today, we'll definitely loose money, know what I'm sayin?

   If the orders do not ship today, we will loose money. Do you understand?

3. Couldn't of gone to the employee lunch if I wanted too. Had too much work.

   It would have been impossible to attend the employee lunch because I had too much work.

4. You better step off and get back to your cubicle and finish your work.

   I think it would be best for you to return to your cubicle and finish your work.

5. Things shoulda gone better if we had been better prepared.

   Things would have gone much better if we had been prepared.

6. That third quarter report is so not there this year.

   The third quarter report is not very good.

7. His administrative assistant is so dizzy.

   His administrative assistance is not very efficient.

8. Don't bet bent outta shape if you don't get the raise you wanted.

   I you do not get the raise, try not to get upset.

9. Last year's Christmas bonuses were the bomb.

   Last year the Christmas bonuses were great.

10. He ditched the meeting and went site seeing instead.

He left the meeting and went site seeing instead.

11. Most of the orders from Europe are very strong and budget projections are off the hook.

The European orders are strong with budget projections looking very positive.

12. When the seminar began, we were distracted. The presenter's dress had way too much bling going on.

We were distracted when the seminar began because the presenter was inappropriately dressed.

13. John stopped worrying about his supervisor busting him cause he was six feet under.

John stopped worrying about getting into trouble at work because his supervisor died.

14. All of the company's management directors want total success but none are prepared to do the heavy lifting.

All of the top executives want success but none are prepared to work themselves.

15. Getting the progress report corrected before the meeting began was a crapshoot.

Getting the progress report corrected before the meeting began was not very likely.

16. Company profits at the end of the quarter were a wash no matter how they tried to spin it.

Even though managers tried to position themselves in a better light, the quarter-end profits were not good.

17. Glenn Baxter's entire proposal for new business was just smoke and mirrors.

Glen Baxter's entire proposal for new business was completely absurd and without merit.

Exercise #4 – Answer Key

October 15, 2012

Mr. John Adams, General Manager
Simmons Automotive
1245 Larsen Blvd
Anderson, MO 63501

Dear Mr. Adams:

We <u>wanna</u> continue to be your customers <u>no matter what</u>. <u>It's</u> been 15 years, maybe more, but <u>who's counting, right?</u> Your company recommended we have a 30,000 mile service on our SUV. Since the service, our vehicle is consistently having trouble starting. Perhaps we should have tried another service, <u>but since you've been around the town so long, we thought we'd come back to you, know what I mean? Anyway, whatever. So getting on with it.</u>

We received a notice from your company to bring our SUV in for service. We did so and were charged $600.00 dollars. Upon signing for the service, I was made aware of your company guarantee that customer satisfaction was the bottom line. It explained your optimum service policy. <u>It went like this.</u> Any customer dissatisfaction would be addressed with a full refund. <u>When I keyed in on this, I thought it was off the hook!</u> But now, I am very disappointed because your customer service person told me to <u>hit the road in so many words. She was pretty dizzy if you know what I mean.</u>

I think you will agree that we have a problem. We were able to secure legal representation and have since taken our SUV to another automotive service. It has been determined that the fuel injection service was not performed and the spark plugs were not replaced. This would account for the failure of our vehicle to start on multiple occasions.

<u>Look buddy, you'll be hearing from our legal peeps. They know what's what when it comes down to handling stuff this messed up.</u> I would like you to authorize another service as soon as possible, or grant a full refund.

Sincerely,

Ronald Cantoni

Answer Key for the Practice Drill—Explanations of the differences between types of tone

THE FIRST SENTENCE: Semi-formal differs from formal with regard to the use of language. Look at the use of the word 'even' in the first sentence of the semi-formal version. This relaxes the tone.

Also, instead of the ultra-formal phrase, "Of the questions that perplex humanity…". There is a simpler version in the semi-formal example, "There are many questions that confuse humanity…". The word, 'confuse' is substituted for the more formal word, 'perplex'.

THE SECOND SENTENCE: The formal version goes like this, "Do we have a spiritual essence…". Compare this to the semi-formal example that uses less words, "What about spirituality?"

THE THIRD SENTENCE: In the formal version, we see "Why does Sex and The City have a reputation for featuring fabulous clothes when the lead actress dresses like an organ grinder's monkey.…etc." In the semi-formal example, there are less words and the tone is considerably friendlier, for instance, "Why is Sex and the City considered all about fashion when the lead actress dresses bad?"

The last sentences in the semi-formal version make it different from the formal version because it uses contractions and fewer, simpler words.

The informal version is very different in tone from the formal and semi-formal versions because it uses a lot of slang, contractions, and wiggle words like 'lotta' and 'weirder'. This version breaks many rules of tone. Check the underlined phrases below.

Tone Errors Found in the Informal version

There are a <u>lotta</u> questions people ask over and over again. <u>Like, what's</u> the meaning of life? Or <u>the craziest one</u>, is reincarnation <u>real or bogus</u>? And <u>the stupidest</u> one about that television program, Sex and the City. Why does Carrie wear clothes <u>that are not all that</u> when the show wants us to believe that the fashion <u>is so on top of it?</u> <u>Who cares really</u>, like whether cat people <u>are weirder</u> than dog people?

Image © Brian A Jackson, 2013. Used under license from Shutterstock, Inc.

THE BUSINESS OF PERSUASION

THE TOULMIN MODEL AND PERSUASIVE BUSINESS WRITING

OVERVIEW

Why Toulmin? Argument is everywhere in business. If you want to succeed or be successful outside of work, learn Toulmin. This argumentation model is based on the work of Stephen Toulmin in his book, The Uses of Argument.

Throughout this book, we will use the Toulmin model to teach you how to write persuasively in the workplace. We will use it in a variety of business documents you may be tasked to write at one time or another. It will help you to understand how you are being persuaded everyday, persuaded to buy ideas, products, or services.

But for now, the job at hand is either your present one or a future one. Regardless, you want to excel at work. Your level of excellence depends on your ability to write persuasively without crafting a twenty page research paper or a formal argumentative essay. This is the beauty of Toulmin, it's a short 'easy to remember' argument model that can be used to create persuasive business documents.

Start to think of any business document **as an argument**. It should have a claim, some thought or belief it is putting forth. It should have support for the claim. It should always address the beliefs and assumptions of your bosses and colleagues. All of these things, claim, support, beliefs and assumptions are part of the Toulmin Model of Argumentation.

When I said argument is everywhere, think about email, memos, business proposals, resumes, and job application letters. All of them can be persuasive. All of them will have something to do with process improvement and problem solving in the workplace.

But remember, even if you're the greatest at solving problems and improving processes, you'll still have to write them down, and you'll still have to sell their value. The only way to do this is to master the art of persuasive business writing, master Toulmin.

> *A Work Scenario:* For instance, if you're solving a problem, you'll need to state it in a proposal. After you state the problem, you have to state the claim, the way you intend to solve the problem. Before you begin to solve the problem by including your support, you have to remember your audience. What are they thinking? What do they believe about the problem? Any preconceived notions at all? These are warrants. You have to be aware of them before you get your support together. When you have a good handle on what going on in the heads of your audience, then you pick your support to cater to their assumptions. All of it has to be logical. It still has to be persuasive, and that is what Toulmin is all about, being logical and persuasive. The same goes for process improvement. So there, I've listed the three main elements of Toulmin: claim, warrants, and support. Let's get to the entire model.

THE SIX ELEMENTS OF THE TOULMIN MODEL

There are six elements in the Toulmin Model. These elements should be present in any business communication designed to persuade: **Claim, Support, Warrants, Backing, Rebuttal, and Qualifiers.**

Figure: 3.1   Six Element of the Toulmin Model - Bubbles

The Claim:

Your claim is the center of the argument. All parts of the argument model are related to the claim. Simply put, your claim is a statement that succinctly describes an idea you want to sell or promote. Generally, if you work in the administrative areas, you will be selling your ideas to colleagues and/or supervisors. These ideas will need to be written in various forms of business documents.

Types of Documents:

- memos
- email
- progress reports
- formal proposals
- workplace letters
- employment correspondence

If you aren't selling yourself by writing employment correspondence to land a job, you probably already have one. If you do, one of the first things you'll learn is that promotions and raises in salary must be earned. What's the best way to earn these things? Be attentive, assertive, and confident enough to look for ways to assure top quality in the workplace.

What's in a Claim? What Does it Do Exactly? In the workplace there is usually a process that needs to be improved or a problem to be solved, or a new idea that will revolutionize the present business model. Whatever the situation at some point in time, you will find yourself in a position tasked with one of these responsibilities: improving a process, solving a problem, or proposing a new business model. Your ideas will need to be written in the form of various types of business documents such as those listed on the previous page. All of these documents must begin with a claim. The claim is the statement by which you propose solutions, improvements, and new models.

Examples of Three Types of Claims in Various Business Arguments

- **Claim for Process Improvement** Presently, our department is closing two purchase orders per hour. The minimum per hour should be four. I am proposing a reduction in reconciliation steps that will increase the number per hour to six.
- **Claim for Solving a Problem** Based on last month's warehouse inventory, there has been an 8 percent increase in shrinkage. Our monthly sales figures do not support this high level of 'missing' merchandise. We cannot afford to hire more security guards. Therefore, I would like to recommend a technological upgrade in our present security system. It will help us accomplish our goals without increasing the payroll.
- **Claim for Changing a Business Model** For the past three fiscal years, our field sales force has used the approach of 'selling on reputation' only. While our company is currently listed in the top three lawn care services, we are not meeting our projected sales goals because there is lack of understanding of client needs. I therefore propose a change in sales approach. I recommend we switch to a 'consultative approach.' It would help our sales force to identify specific needs, make recommendations to service those needs and quickly close the sale.

The Warrants:

Warrants are the same as 'audience'. This is a very important element in the Toulmin model because it helps you address what your reader is thinking. Warrants are the unstated values, thoughts, assumptions, and commonly held beliefs in the minds of your bosses and/or colleagues. They can be put into words and will become part of your written document. Think of your bosses and colleagues as your audience. Warrants are absolutely crucial for the success of your argument. Warrants are all of the things your audience believes about whatever idea you are promoting. Most of the time, they will not share these thoughts with you. Always remember they carry these things internally and they will influence their decision making.

How Can You Figure out the Boss's Warrants? First, you must be diligent on the job. You must keep your ears open, stay informed, and stay engaged with co-workers on job related issues. Second, you must be aware of your boss's 'success objectives.' Success Objectives are specific things that must be achieved to demonstrate a successful department or project team. In plain language, your supervisor or manager will always want to meet these to look great, keep their jobs and yours, get raises in salary or receive promotions.

> **Here's How Warrants Work**: If you want to convince your supervisor to give you a shorter work week for the same pay, you'll need to understand why she wouldn't want to give you a shorter work week. In other words, you must figure out what she thinks about shorter work weeks. This is where you begin to make assumptions. These assumptions or guesses are **warrants**. Again, warrants are the same as AUDIENCE. Do not be confused by the term.

When you have a strong idea of what may be going on in the mind of your supervisor or co-workers, you will have a strong idea of how to build your argument. Building your argument starts with creating a foundation upon which the argument roots with WARRANTS or audience being the center weight bearing pier. All together, the foundation is supported by three piers: Claim, Support, and Warrants. For now, we will focus on warrants.

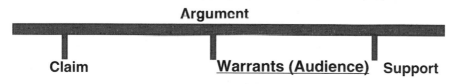

Argument

| Claim | **Warrants (Audience)** | Support |

Figure: 3.2   Agument-Claim, Warrants, Support

Some Examples of Unstated Warrants that Support the Three Types of Claims

Claim for Process Improvement Presently, our department is closing two purchase orders per hour. The minimum per hour should be four. I am proposing a reduction in reconciliation steps that will increase the number per hour to six.

- **Warrants (Audience)**: The facility manager distributes a monthly newsletter that highlights shrinkage and how it decreases company profits. You know your supervisor keeps a close eye on this issue and measures warehouse shrinkage monthly, then reports this to the facility manger. You also know that your supervisor constantly talks about adding more technology and wants to be noticed by the facility manager. You also know that the facility manager would like to avoid hiring more security personnel.

Claim for Changing a Business Model   For the past three fiscal years, our field sales force has used the approach of 'selling on reputation' only. While our company is currently listed in the top three lawn care services, we are not meeting our projected sales goals because there is lack of understanding of client needs. I therefore propose a change in sales approach. I recommend we switch to a 'consultative approach.' It would help our sales force to identify specific needs, make recommendations to service those needs and quickly close the sale.

- **Warrants:** The District Sales Manager is your immediate supervisor. You understand it is likely he will lay-off people in your area if the district sales figures do not improve. During weekly staff meetings, the district manager always includes 'new sales approaches' on the agenda. You are also well aware of the fact that the district manager reports to an area Vice President of Sales. This Area VP always includes a section on new training initiatives in her quarterly newsletter.

HOW TO WRITE WARRANTS INTO A BUSINESS DOCUMENT.

Example: If you were writing a memo to your boss arguing a change in sales approach. You would need to include at least 4 essential Toulmin elements: backing, claim, support, and warrants. Read and study the example on the adjacent page.

1. **Backing**
2. **Claim**
3. **Support**
4. **Warrants**

To: Bill Cutter, District Mgr
From: Jack Carlton
Date: November 6, 2012
Subject: Change in Sales Approach for Field Sales Personnel

(1) Backing: For the past three fiscal years, our field sales force has used the approach of 'selling on reputation' only. While our company is currently listed in the top three lawn care services, we are not meeting our projected sales goals because there is lack of understanding of client needs. Claim:

(2) I therefore propose a change in sales approach. I recommend we switch to a 'consultative approach'. It would help our sales force to identify specific needs, make recommendations to service those needs and quickly close the sale.

(3) Support: Last quarter's sales figures reflected a 23% drop in revenue. Most clients pointed out that our field sales people rarely asked questions about their business needs. In other words, sales personnel are not being aggressive and specific when it comes to client needs. As a result, we continue to miss opportunities to sell our products.

(4) Warrants: It is clear that lay-offs are likely to occur if the district sales figures do not improve. You cover this possibility in our weekly staff meetings. I feel it would be advantageous for us to formally ask for training funds and re-shape our sales approach. This will undoubtedly improve our sales figures, your relationship with the area VP, and avoid lay-offs. I am sure you can see how all parties will benefit.

Let me know your thoughts.

Figure 3.3   Typical Memo Using the Toulmin Model.

These were previously unstated warrants in the mind of the district manager. Now they are explicitly stated in the memo and are called Warrants. This is how you address unstated warrants in your argument.

FURTHER EXAMPLES OF WARRANTS If you were writing memos based on claims that solve problems, they would include the 3 essential Toulmin elements.

Scenario #1: *You are an assistant operations manger at a factory that manufactures metal storage buildings. You are failing to make your weekly quota. You write a memo to your boss to solve this problem.*

Your Claim: The normal work day should be increased from 8 hours to 10 hours.

Your Support: Over time payroll costs will be reduced.

Warrants: Your boss would probably think that it is good to increase productivity without raising payroll. He has mentioned it a staff meetings. Workers can put in an extra two hours per day without the company having to pay overtime.

If you were writing these warrants in a memo, your final 'warrants' paragraph would read something like this:

Employee overtime will cause a rise in payroll expense which would offset any gains in productivity. Increasing the work day from eight to ten hours will solve this problem. It will eliminate two hours of overtime expense, yet improve productivity with two additional hours of straight time.

Scenario #2: *You are an employee at a local retail store. The rate of muggings and car burglaries has increased in the last three months. You and your co-workers do not feel safe. You have been chosen to write a memo to the manager.*

Your Claim: The employee parking lot should be made more secure after hours.

Your Support: Three cars have been burglarized within one month.

Warrants: Your boss will more than likely be concerned about the safety of employees. He or she would be more likely to increase security which would ensure safety. The generally held belief in this case would be Republicans do not work well with Democrats on legislation.

If you were writing these warrants in a memo, your final 'warrants' paragraph would read something like this:

I am sure you agree that the safety of all employees should be a top priority given the recent crimes taking place in the parking lot. Because our parent company would have to assume liability in these cases, adding security cameras and increasing lighting in the parking lot would be a sound idea.

The Support:

This will be the evidence that will convince your bosses or colleagues to accept your claim. You will need quantifiable support and non-quantifiable support. Both work in tandem and are acceptable to use in any persuasive business document. The way in which you use support is up to you and should be strategic. Think about warrants. Knowing how your audience or your supervisor feels about whatever problem you want to solve or whatever process you want to improve is important. Or, in plain language, knowing what's going on in the minds of your supervisors will help you figure out what will be the best type of support. So remember, warrants drive support.

How does this work? Here's a scenario: *You work in the Human Resources Department. You are in charge of monitoring and disseminating information sent to the HR suggestion box. For a long time you have wanted to change the way employees are hired. You do not feel that the decision should come down to one person. You have finally decided to write a memo to the Manger of Human Resources.*

Claim – Process Improvement: Employees should be hired using a 'hiring committee' rather than a hiring manager.

Warrants – You know that the Manger has received many complaints in the suggestion box that deal with unfair hiring practices. There is a growing dissatisfaction among employees. It appears that department mangers are hiring people for things other than qualifications. You know your manager does not like to be the first to make a change that is unproven.

Support – Because you know your manger does not like to be the 'first' to initiate change, you have researched the 'hiring committee' process. You have found that this is the customary practice in academia and is fast becoming a new process in corporate America. You will gather examples of specific companies and universities that use this practice. You will gather statistics that measure numbers of new employees hired using this process. You will gather expert opinions in the field of human resources that support the 'hiring committee' and any projections for continued use.

TYPES OF SUPPORT   Quantifiable Support

- Facts
- Statistics
- Examples
- Reasoning

Non-Quantifiable Support   Personal Opinions and Recommendations
Expert Opinions and Recommendations

The Backing:

Sometimes warrants are in danger of being rejected. If so, you need to have their 'back.' This is the first of the three optional Toulmin elements called 'backing.' Think of them as them as support for the warrants because warrants sometimes need extra defense. Backing can be written into the document as well. Backing is a strategy that supports the warrants of your audience to your advantage. Both go hand in hand, information that speaks to your supervisor's basic beliefs, values, commonly held truths about specific business issues. You would include this information in your business document only if you think your supervisor may reject your warrants.

Here's an example of 'backing' for a warrant.

Your Claim: The employee parking lot should be made more secure after hours.

Your Support: Three cars have been burglarized within one month.

Warrants: I am sure you agree that the safety of all employees should be a top priority given the recent crimes taking place in the parking lot. Because our parent company would have to assume liability in these cases, adding security cameras and increasing lighting in the parking lot would be a sound idea.

Backing: On average, liability claims can range from $10,000 to $50,000. In cases that involve criminal acts and victimization, the awards can double.

The Rebuttal:

This is also an optional Toulmin element. Rebuttals expose possible weaknesses in your argument by addressing them and disabling them. You are countering an anticipated objection to your proposal or recommendation. If a colleague or boss fails to be persuaded by your argument, the support may lack strength or the warrants may be inaccurate. To avoid a 'denial' of your plan or solution, you must anticipate the weak areas in your proposal.

Here's an example for rebuttals using the claim above....

> A weak spot your boss might point out in your proposal: State
> of the art security systems are expensive and would require an
> overall upgrade to the building electrical schematic in addition
> to enhancements in the parking lot. An investment of this size at
> this time is not possible.

In your argument, you would address this weakness before your boss has
a chance to deny your proposal. To avoid this, address the weak area by
writing your rebuttal in your document.

Your Rebuttal

> Installing security enhancements in the parking lot would more
> than likely require additional upgrades to the store itself. These
> would only be enhancements and would not require a completely
> new security system and new wiring. The security upgrades would
> amount to 30% of the cost of a completely new system. The 70%
> savings would be a good investment in avoiding future law suits.

So far, here's the framework for your argument using five of the six Toulmin elements....

> **Your Claim:** The employee parking lot should be made more secure
> after hours.
>
> **Your Support:** Three cars have been burglarized within one month.
>
> **Warrants:** I am sure you agree that the safety of all employees
> should be a top priority given the recent crimes taking place in the
> parking lot. Because our parent company would have to assume
> liability in these cases, adding security cameras and increasing light-
> ing in the parking lot would be a sound idea.
>
> **Backing:** On average, liability claims can range from $10,000 to
> $50,000. In cases that involve criminal acts and victimization, the
> awards can double.
>
> **Rebuttal:** Costs: Installing security enhancements in the parking lot
> would more than likely require additional upgrades to the store itself.
> These would only be enhancements and would not require a com-
> pletely new security system and new wiring. The security upgrades
> would amount to 30% of the cost of a completely new system. The
> 70% savings would be a good investment in avoiding future law suits.

The best way to sniff out weak spots in your argument where rebuttals
are concerned is to ask yourself these questions. "Are there any other ways
to address this problem or improve this process? What are the costs in
either manpower or dollars?

If you answer yes to these questions, research the alternatives and compare to your own plan. If your plan is the best, do not be afraid to write the rebuttals into your argument. But be strategic with regard to where you place them. If you uncover alternative solutions that would improve your plan, think of ways to incorporate them. Sometimes, great ideas can use a little help.

The Qualifier:

Qualifiers are words or language that will not pin you down to a certainty. Remember, there are no guarantees in the business world, thus no guarantee that your proposal, report, or letter will absolutely 'change the world.' Do not use words in your document like 'always' 'absolutely' 'never.' Use words like maybe, sometimes, might, could, probably, or possibly. This is called qualified language. Using qualified language is much safer than absolutely stating that your ideas or proposals will absolutely work in all situations.

Here's the frame work of your argument using all six Toulmin elements....

Your Claim: The employee parking lot should be made more secure after hours.

Your Support: Three cars have been burglarized within one month.

Warrants: I am sure you agree that the safety of all employees should be a top priority given the recent crimes taking place in the parking lot. Because our parent company would have to assume liability in these cases, adding security cameras and increasing lighting in the parking lot would be a sound idea.

Backing: On average, liability claims can range from $10,000 to $50,000. In cases that involve criminal acts and victimization, the awards can double.

Rebuttal: Costs: Installing security enhancements in the parking lot would more than likely require additional upgrades to the store itself. These would only be enhancements and would not require a completely new security system and new wiring. The security upgrades would amount to 30% of the cost of a completely new system. The 70% savings would be a good investment in avoiding future law suits.

Qualifier: While updating the security system in the parking area will certainly decrease risk with regard to employee safety; it is not an absolute deterrent. It is however, a short term means to limit liability for the store.

SECTION 3 RECAP:

Why Toulmin? You want to be successful, that's why. Whether you're bound for the sciences or the business world, achieving prosperity is part of what we understand as success.

Being able to shape and communicate your ideas in a cohesive and persuasive manner is essential. It's strange to think that business documents or scientific papers are arguments. Essentially, they are. Think about their purpose. I have already cited the three big areas with which you will be faced on the job.

Problem Solution

Process Improvement

Change of Business Model

To achieve any of these would require an effective argument. Let's face it, persuasion will be part of your work life. To review, the six elements of Toulmin:

- **The Claim** – This is the problem you want to solve, the process you want to improve, or the model you want to change.
- **The Support** – This is the data, the facts, the examples, the statistics, the opinions you will need to give your claim validity.
- **The Warrants** – These are the unstated positions of your bosses or colleagues that will influence their decision making. Think of warrants as 'audience psychology.' Understand your audience and you'll understand how to frame your argument.
- **The Backing** – This is data that backs up warrants. Backing is optional. You do not always have to have extra information that will cause your warrants to be stronger.
- **Rebuttals** – These are also optional. They expose any weaknesses that may be in your argument. Including rebuttals will defuse any counter arguments.
- **Qualifiers** – Qualifying language is also optional. Using it will give you some 'wiggle-room' with regard to the correctness of your ideas. Qualifying language will keep you from being pinned down for specific outcomes.

Please Complete the Following Exercises for Section 3. Answer Keys will follow.

Exercise #1:

The letter below is an inquiry for employment. There are four Toulmin Elements embedded in the body: claim, support, warrants, and backing. Locate these elements and underline.

November 15, 2012

Janet Aldrich, Director of Human Resources
Maersk Shipping Lines
1 Commercial Plaza
Norfolk, VA 23510

Dear Ms. Aldrich:

Subject: **Inquiry - Logistics Manager Position with Maersk**

Operations Management, International Marketing, International Trade and Finance, Cross-Cultural Communication, International Business Management: I believe these courses alongside an internship and pertinent employment have given me the essential skills and experience employers would seek.

My experience includes: export documentation, creating international bills of lading for global accounts, loading shipping containers, and performing commercial merchant ship procedures. Your company will benefit from an employee that is experienced in both administration and operations.

With my internship and employment at APL Lines, I have learned shipping routes, restrictions and ratings for goods, insurance, and arrival times. Through my employment as a dock worker, I learned the commercial ship's design, speed, crew compliment, manifestation, and how to load and secure shipping containers.

My references will validate my knowledge, work ethic, and discipline. I am prepared to accomplish any task put before me. If an opening is available, I would gladly accept an interview at your convenience.

Sincerely,

John M. Jacobs

Encl: Resume

Exercise #1 – Answer Key

1. Warrants – The writer wants to highlight the skills he believes the employer would desire in an applicant. **THIS IS A WARRANT** because the writer is making assumptions about the employers beliefs. He then makes the connection between these skills he thinks the employer deems valuable and himself.
2. Focusing on his experience and relying on his skills previously stated, the writer plainly asks for a job. **Claim**
3. Relates information from resume to employer's needs. **THIS IS SUPPORT.**
4. This **IS BACKING.** The writer continues to support the main warrant with his relevant personal traits.

November 15, 2012

Janet Aldrich, Director of Human Resources
Maersk Shipping Lines
1 Commercial Plaza
Norfolk, VA 23510

Dear Ms. Aldrich:

Subject: **Inquiry - Logistics Manager Position with Maersk**

(1) Operations Management, International Marketing, International Trade and Finance, Cross-Cultural Communication, International Business Management: I believe these courses alongside an internship and pertinent employment have given me the essential skills and experience employers would seek.

(2) My experience includes: export documentation, creating international bills of lading for global accounts, loading shipping containers, and performing commercial merchant ship procedures. Your company will benefit from an employee that is experienced in both administration and operations.

(3) With my internship and employment at APL Lines, I have learned shipping routes, restrictions and ratings for goods, insurance, and arrival times. Through my employment as a dock worker, I learned the commercial ship's design, speed, crew compliment, manifestation, and how to load and secure shipping containers.

(4) My references will validate my knowledge, work ethic, and discipline. I am prepared to accomplish any task put before me. If an opening is available, I would gladly accept an interview at your convenience.

Sincerely,

John M. Jacobs

Encl: Resume

Exercise #2:

The email below is a justification email. There are four Toulmin Elements embedded in the body. Locate these elements and underline.

From: Martin Hillcrest, Human Resources - Houston
To: Carl Martin, Corporate Human Resources
CC: Jane Stevens, Director of Operations - Houston

Subject: **Designated Smoking Areas**

Hi Carl,

Thank you for considering designated smoking areas on our campus. Your cooperation reinforces the goodwill between employee and employer.

I am convinced our company values its public image as well as its commitment to wellness. I am also aware that having smoking areas is a luxury. My concern is that these designated smoking areas are too visible to our clients and visitors.

I worry our clients and visitors may be adversely affected by second hand smoke particularly because the areas are adjacent to the main entrance. We may want to reconsider the locations of these areas right away. They may cause a long lasting negative impression.

Wellness is not only a company issue but a public one. I am sure you understand that the image we project must be positive. Keeping our clients and non-smoking employees in mind, I would suggest we move the designated smoking areas to the rear of the building at least twenty feet from the employee entrance. This should satisfy all parties.

Let me know what you think.

Martin Hillcrest

Human Resources - Houston
ENG Technology, Inc
888-222-1111
asomorin@engtech.org

Exercise #2 – Answer Key

1. Warrant – The writer is opening with a positive. He is assuming his boss wants to keep goodwill between the company and its employees and decides to address it explicitly.
2. Claim – The writer clearly states what problem he wishes to solve. He 'claims' the smoking areas are miss-placed.
3. Support – Evidence to support a problem with existing smoking areas.
4. Warrants – The writer is making assumptions about what his boss believes with regard to image and wellness. When the writer addresses these assumptions, the warrants move from being unstated in the mind of the audience or the boss to explicit warrants in the document itself.

From: Martin Hillcrest, Human Resources - Houston
To: Carl Martin, Corporate Human Resources
CC: Jane Stevens, Director of Operations - Houston

Subject: **Designated Smoking Areas**

Hi Carl,

(1) Thank you for considering designated smoking areas on our campus. Your cooperation reinforces the goodwill between employee and employer.

(2) I am convinced our company values its public image as well as its commitment to wellness. I am also aware that having smoking areas is a luxury. My concern is that these designated smoking areas are too visible to our clients and visitors.

(3) I worry our clients and visitors may be adversely affected by second hand smoke particularly because the areas are adjacent to the main entrance. We may want to reconsider the locations of these areas right away. They may cause a long lasting negative impression.

(4) Wellness is not only a company issue but a public one. I am sure you understand that the image we project must be positive. Keeping our clients and non-smoking employees in mind, I would suggest we move the designated smoking areas to the rear of the building at least twenty feet from the employee entrance. This should satisfy all parties.

Let me know what you think.

Martin Hillcrest

Human Resources - Houston
ENG Technology, Inc
888-222-1111
asomorin@engtech.org

Image © Nata-Lia, 2013. Used under license from Shutterstock, Inc.

WHAT HAPPENED TO THE MEMO?

…IS IT EMAIL OR WHAT?

Section 4 will address the 'how to' when it comes to writing persuasive memos and persuasive email.

PERSUASIVE MEMOS

It can be hard to tell the difference between the traditional memo and an email message. Memos frequently do not have the 'MEMORANDUM' banner at the top anymore. They are frequently sent in the form of an email or as an email attachment. So, is it email or what? No, memos are not email. They are longer. They can use various techniques to layout information such as: bullets, sub-headings, and the occasional table if it is very small. In short, memos include much more detailed information. They are a more formal document.

We will look at persuasive memos first and then the persuasive email. The purpose of this section is to point out the 'not so obvious.' Most people do not think of memos as anything other than simple messages, miscellaneous bits of information. Possibly, but you should ask yourself, what is your end goal? Let's take a giant leap and assume you want to be successful, get promotions, have your ideas accepted and applauded, receive pay raises and maybe even a reserved parking spot. If this is close to what you imagine your professional life should be, then begin to think of memos and all other business writing as persuasive documents.

The catch is this, you must write them persuasively. You must argue much in a small amount of space. Your manager or supervisor will have little time to read through many documents during the day. Typically, they should be able to digest a persuasive memo in 5 minutes. This requires real skill. You must understand that it is up to you to turn a simple business document like a memo into a concise effective argument that will cause your audience to change positions or accept whatever it is you are proposing better know as your claim or proposition.

What Do Persuasive Memos Do?

- To convince and push to action
- To propose directives through summary and analysis
- To report and make recommendations
- To generate or solidify interest through

FORM AND FUNCTION

Function

Typically, they are sent via email and should focus on one topic. They should also be kept to one page. Your audience will have a short attention span. Persuasive memos will always impart information, but it is the way in which they impart the information that matters. They can put forth a claim or proposition to solve a problem, improve a process, justify or announce changes or updates in a manner that encourages acceptance, and recap events in a manner that implies success.

Form

- Memos should be kept to 1 – 1 ½ pages.
- Use an easy to read font, generally 12' is acceptable
- Strive to keep them to one page.
- Margins should be 1 inch all around.
- Paragraphs are always single-spaced.

- Initial your typed signature in the heading.
- The paragraphs are never indented.
- The opening paragraph should contain the claim or proposition.
- The body should provide details or support.
- The closing paragraphs always contain warrants.

GUIDELINES for Writing Persuasive Memos

- **Ask Yourself** – Decide the purpose of your document and pick the correct type of memo.
- **The Distribution** – Make sure you distribute to the right people.
- **Interoffice Only** – Use memos for internal purposes only.
- **Craft your argument wisely** – Use the most important evidence.
- **Keep your language simple** – Do not use ten-dollar words or overly embellished phrases.
- **Be Concise** – Strive for economy of words. You will have limited space to pose your argument.
- **Think Audience** – Always be aware of your audience. Write for them taking certain things into consideration such as: Who are they? What are their expectations?
- **Tone** – Keep an appropriate tone. Go with formal or semi-formal depending on your relationship with your colleagues.
- **Organization** – Sketch out a short outline of your paragraphs. You should have no more than three or four. Make sure they are organized in an easy to follow, easy to understand manner. They must flow into each other logically.
- **Proofread** – Always check your grammar and spelling. Do not leave red/green lines visible in your document. Run a spell/grammar check. If the spelling or grammar appears to be correct. Hit the 'add to dictionary' button, or 'ignore rule' button.
- **White Space** – Manage your white space. Bullets and sub-headings are acceptable. Tables are not generally used in memos. They will consume too much white space.

NOTES

A STANDARD MEMO

MEMORANDUM

To: Audio-Video Division Team Leaders, Kansas City Office
From: Carl Hatfield, Procurement Manager
Date: January 12, 2013

Subject: **New Editing Software – Selection Process**

Per our conversations on the purchase of new editing software, I have researched several manufacturers. It is clear that our needs outweigh our budget. But at the risk of sacrificing quality for cost, I did not disqualify any of the versions for price only. I compared the technical features of the software, support, and compatibility.

I narrowed the list to three providers: Bennetton, Crayson, and Showzone. I managed to stay within the department budget. Bennetton is priced at $4,400. Crayson is priced at $5,200, and Showzone is priced at $4,695. I have prepared a product brief on each of the software packages for your review. I have already made an initial determination of which version will support our department and manage to keep within budget constraints. However, your input is most important.

Please study the product briefs carefully. Take time to make clear notes on each so that I will be able to sift through your findings. Afterward, select your top two and return all your notes to me via email. I will review your findings and select the top pick. I will contact you with the results as quickly as possible. If the selection meets with everyone's approval, I will order the software.

Thanks in advance for your help. Time is precious and busy schedules are always a priority. As a company and as a department team, the spirit of cooperation always ensures success.

cc: Allison Cooper
    Bart Madison

Legend

1. Title: Memo, Memorandum, or Interoffice Memo.
2. Heading
3. Subject Line
4. *Claim* which is also a directive to action.
5. Opening Paragraph should contain sentences that orient your reader to the subject. Your *claim* or proposition is located in this paragraph.
6. Body Paragraph – Support should be located here. Research, data, any material needed for your audience to proceed.
7. Conclusion – You give your audience instructions for the process and some idea of when a response will be received.
8. Statement of Thanks

PARTS OF A STANDARD MEMO

MEMORANDUM —①

To: Audio-Video Division Team Leaders, Kansas City Office
②—From: Carl Hatfield, Procurement Manager
Date: January 12, 2013

Subject: **New Editing Software – Selection Process** —③

④—*It is necessary that our editing software be updated. It will be necessary for you to contribute to this process.* To that end, I have researched several manu-
⑤—facturers. At the risk of sacrificing quality for cost, I did not disqualify any of the versions for price only. I compared the technical features of the software, support, and compatibility.

I narrowed the list to three providers: Bennetton, Crayson, and Showzone. I managed to stay within the department budget. Bennetton is priced at $4,400. Crayson is priced at $5,200, and Showzone is priced at $4, 695.
⑥—I have prepared a product brief on each of the software packages for your review. I have already made an initial determination of which version will support our department and manage to keep within budget constraints. However, your input is most important.

Please study the product briefs carefully. Take time to make clear notes on each so that I will be able to sift through your findings. Afterward,
⑦—select your top two and return all your notes to me via email. I will review your findings and select the top pick. I will contact you with the results as quickly as possible. If the selection meets with everyone's approval, I will order the software.

Thanks in advance for your help. Time is precious and busy schedules are
⑧—always a priority. As a company and as a department team, the spirit of cooperation always ensures success.

cc: Allison Cooper
    Bart Madison

Legend

1. The entire memo should be left justified. Right margins set ragged edge, not justified.
2. Memorandum line should be 3 line spaces from the top margin default of 1" or 8 – 10 line spaces from the top edge of the paper.
3. There should be 3 line spaces between the document title and the heading.
4. Heading is single spaced. There should be 1 inch between the colon and heading information [to, from, date]
5. There should be 2 line spaces between the heading and the subject line
6. Subject line should be kept to one line and 'bold'.
7. There should be 2 line spaces between the subject line and the opening paragraph.
8. All body paragraphs should be single spaced with no indents.
9. There should be 1 line space between each single spaced body paragraph.
10. 1 line space between the 'statement of thanks' and the courtesy copy notation.

STANDARD MEMO WITH SPACING GUIDLINES

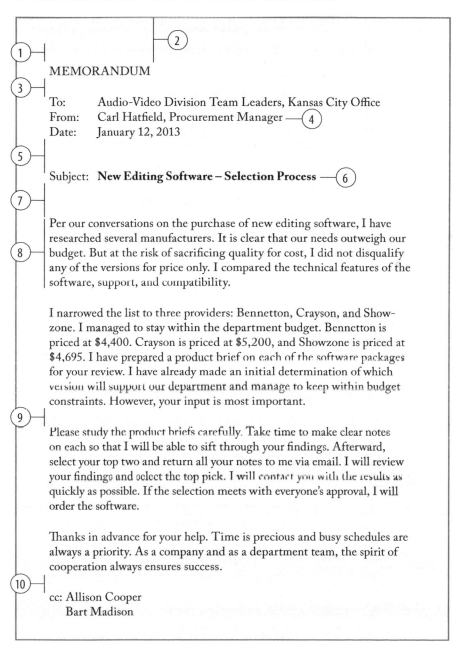

MEMORANDUM

To: Audio-Video Division Team Leaders, Kansas City Office
From: Carl Hatfield, Procurement Manager
Date: January 12, 2013

Subject: **New Editing Software – Selection Process**

Per our conversations on the purchase of new editing software, I have
researched several manufacturers. It is clear that our needs outweigh our
budget. But at the risk of sacrificing quality for cost, I did not disqualify
any of the versions for price only. I compared the technical features of the
software, support, and compatibility.

I narrowed the list to three providers: Bennetton, Crayson, and Showzone. I managed to stay within the department budget. Bennetton is
priced at $4,400. Crayson is priced at $5,200, and Showzone is priced at
$4,695. I have prepared a product brief on each of the software packages
for your review. I have already made an initial determination of which
version will support our department and manage to keep within budget
constraints. However, your input is most important.

Please study the product briefs carefully. Take time to make clear notes
on each so that I will be able to sift through your findings. Afterward,
select your top two and return all your notes to me via email. I will review
your findings and select the top pick. I will contact you with the results as
quickly as possible. If the selection meets with everyone's approval, I will
order the software.

Thanks in advance for your help. Time is precious and busy schedules are
always a priority. As a company and as a department team, the spirit of
cooperation always ensures success.

cc: Allison Cooper
    Bart Madison

3 TYPES OF PERSUASIVE MEMOS

This section will focus on **THREE** useful persuasive memos. They can be used within the company or outside the company. They are all designed to be persuasive using elements from the Toulmin Model of Argumentation.

The Standard Memo *announces proposed changes in a manner that will persuade an audience to accept those changes*

The Justification Memo *puts forth an argument to solve a problem or improve a process*

The Recap Memo *recaps events/meetings in a manner that will persuade an audience of future success*

THE CHARACTERISTICS

Persuasive memos that use the Toulmin Model of Argumentation should have three characteristics. Let's refer to them as the PMB.

Purpose *A desired effect, a goal or intended outcome*

Message *Persuasive communication using the Toulmin model*

Benefit *Something that you will gain, as a result of the document.*

All persuasive memos will have PMB: *a purpose, a convincing message, and a worthwhile benefit* outlined on the *PMB* page. Each memo will be presented in two formats: a read-only version and a version with highlighted Toulmin Elements. Before we study these memos, we will need to review Toulmin, a typical memo, the basic parts of a typical memo, and the basic format of a typical memo.

The Six Elements of the Toulmin Model

Memos can use some or all of these elements. Because memos are typically brief and kept to one page, you may have to reduce your use of the elements. **The minimum is three. You must always have a claim, support, and warrants**. The other elements are optional and will depend on the kind of argument you wish to put forth. Review the elements below.

- **The Claim**: This is the proposition in any business document. This will be what the document wants you to buy, believe, or do.
- **The Support/Data**: This will be the evidence that will persuade you to accept the claim. Things like opinions, reasons, examples, facts, data, information, and statistics.
- **The Warrants**: Warrants are very interesting and very important to the art of persuasion. They are intangibles for the most part. These are things that your audience believes about certain issues. The easiest way to describe them is to call them assumptions,

widely held values, commonly accepted beliefs, cultural values, and generally accepted truths. Always remember that your audience will carry these things internally and they will drive his or her ability to accept what you are proposing.

- **The Backing**: Backing is a strategy that supports the warrants of your audience to your advantage. They go hand in hand. This would be information included in your document that speaks to your audiences' basic beliefs, values, commonly held truths about specific issues. You would include this information in your business document only if you have a strong sense of your audiences' warrants. **Optional**
- **The Rebuttal**: Exposing anticipated counter-arguments or possible weaknesses in your proposal, letter, or other business communication is called a rebuttal. If you are countering an anticipated argument, include information to refute it. If you are addressing your argument's possible weaknesses, shore them up. 'A good defense is sometimes a good offense'. **Strongly Suggested**.
- **The Qualifier**: Qualifiers are words or language that will not pin you down to a certainty. Remember, there are no guarantees in the business world, thus no guarantee that your proposal, report, or letter will absolutely 'change the world.' Do not use words in your document like 'always' 'absolutely' 'never'. Use words like maybe, sometimes, might, could, probably, or possibly. **Optional**

THE STANDARD MEMO

When Do You Write a Standard Memo?

The Occasion arises when there is an impending update, organizational changes, announcements, or miscellaneous news that must be justified.

What's the PMB?

The Purpose A standard memo is not just to impart information. It should be inherently persuasive. It should be designed to inform and convince. It will put forth a proposition. A proposition or claim always has purpose. When a document has a purpose, it has an audience to convince. When you are convincing an audience, you are persuading. The business audience always needs justification.

The Message The message should mask an argument. The message will be simple in this type of memo. Keep it brief. You will need at no more than three paragraphs. The opening paragraph should contain the claim or proposition. The second paragraph should contain the support for the claim, the content that will convince or justify the information being put forth.

The Benefit The benefit of writing a general information memo with an argumentative model is acceptance. As stated earlier, business audiences need justification for change.

Two Examples of a Standard Memo to follow:

- An unmarked version for study
- A marked version to study the positioning and explanation of Toulmin elements within the document.

MEMORANDUM

To: All Department Managers
From: Dean Miller, Manager of Human Resources
Date: March 6, 20XX

Subject: **Corporate Recycling Program**

As you know, corporate has decided to institute a recycling program in all branch offices. Thomason Industries has decided to support the national initiative to go 'green' and maintain an environmentally conscious position. There will be two recycle containers in each break room. The recycled items will be plastic and cans. There will also be an extra disposal container in each office work space to recycle used paper. Why?

Due to climate change, landfill issues, and the overuse of natural resources in general, corporate intends to support efforts to lessen the impact in whatever way possible. Branch offices are situated in local communities, towns, and cities that are instituting various recycling programs. Thomason Industries intends to be a part of these community efforts. In the long term, it will be good for the environment, good for community relations, and good for business. All three are indelibly tied together.

Please stop by Human Resources for more details. Because the majority of Americans believe in recycling and take an active interest in protecting the environment, we expect 100% participation. This program will not cost any employee anything other than the few seconds it takes to toss a can into the can container, or used paper into the paper container. The cost is nil, the benefit is great. A strong corporate position that supports the environment will help all employees and the globe in the long run.

Thanks

cc: Ralph Smith, V.P. Corporate Human Resources
     Loren Miller, V.P. Operations

Figure: 4.1 Sample   Standard Memo

Legend

1. **Claim** – Where the writer states the upcoming program. The writer is making a case, an argument of sorts that he ultimately wants his audience to accept.
2. **Support** – This is the evidence with which the writer hopes to convince the audience that the claim or proposition is valid and beneficial to the corporation.
3. **Warrants** – This is the closing paragraph where the writer addresses the unstated beliefs of his audience: cost and benefits. This is also a rebuttal because it poses a counter argument for those who may feel the program has no value.

MEMORANDUM

To: All Department Managers
From: Dean Miller, Manager of Human Resources
Date: March 6, 20XX

Subject: **Corporate Recycling Program**

As you know, corporate has decided to institute a recycling program
in all branch offices. Thomason Industries has decided to support the
national initiative to go 'green' and maintain an environmentally conscious
position. There will be two recycle containers in each break room. The
recycled items will be plastic and cans. There will also be an extra disposal
container in each office work space to recycle used paper. Why?

Due to climate change, landfill issues, and the overuse of natural resources
in general, corporate intends to support efforts to lessen the impact in
whatever way possible. Branch offices are situated in local communities,
towns, and cities that are instituting various recycling programs. Thomason Industries intends to be a part of these community efforts. In the long
term, it will be good for the environment, good for community relations,
and good for business. All three are indelibly tied together.

Please stop by Human Resources for more details. Because the majority
of Americans believe in recycling and take an active interest in protecting
the environment, we expect 100% participation. This program will not
cost any employee anything other than the few seconds it takes to toss a
can into the can container, or used paper into the paper container. The cost
is nil, the benefit is great. A strong corporate position that supports the
environment will help all employees and the globe in the long run.

Thanks

cc: Ralph Smith, V.P. Corporate Human Resources
    Loren Miller, V.P. Operations

Figure: 4.2 Toulmin Placement   This version gives positioning and explanation of the Toulmin elements.

THE JUSTIFICATION MEMO

When Do You Write a Justification Memo?

The Occasion arises when there is a process to be improved or a problem to be solved.

What's the PMB?

The Purpose A justification memo is a formal argument. It can also be thought of as a very brief proposal. It has a two-fold purpose. It will put forth a problem that must be solved or a process that must be improved. And it will convince the audience that the solution or new process should be accepted.

The Message The entire memo should be kept to one page. You will be tempted to exceed. Do not do this. Your audience has a short attention span when it comes to memos and email. Be brief. This is the challenge.

The message should contain at least five Toulmin elements. The body should contain sub-headings for three sections: background and recommendation, benefits and costs, and the conclusion. The background/recommendation area will contain the claim and backing. The benefits and costs section will contain the support and the rebuttal. The conclusion which is the final paragraph will contain the warrants. You may include bullet points if necessary. Tables are not a good idea. It will take up too much white space. Your white space is best used for your argument.

The Benefit The obvious benefit is the acceptance of your proposed solution or new process. Remember this. Ultimately, acceptance will depend on the quality of your argument. Take time to adequately research. Be logical in your approach. Be concise. Keep an appropriate tone.

Two Examples of a Justification Memo to follow:

- An unmarked version for study
- A marked version to study the placement of Toulmin elements and focus on the argument in the document

MEMORANDUM

To: Jim Myers, President, Uptown Jazz Café, Inc.
From: Bill Wyatt, Manager, Uptown Jazz Café, Houston,
Date: February 11, April 18, 2013

Subject: **Need to Increase Wait Staff**

Background and Recommendation
Our Houston store, Uptown Jazz Café, Beacon Street is not meeting its 3rd quarter projections. Having only 12 wait staff, service to our patrons has suffered. As a result, our business has shrunk by 30%.

To increase business as well as meet our quarterly sales goals, I recommend that we hire four additional servers, two additional cooks, and one additional dishwasher. Additional staff will be able to meet our needs on three fronts: service, food quality, and sanitation.

Benefits and Costs
Seven full-time staff will have a positive effect on our business.

- Dirty plates, glassware, and eating utensils will not pile up. Tables will be bused faster.
- Staff will not be called on to work additional hours and will cut down on overtime and work fatigue.
- Waiting time to seat patrons will be decreased.
- Attention to customers will be increased.
- Food to table wait time will be decreased.
- Food Quality will be improved with a greater number of cooks to share the order load.

Costs: Initial projections for wages would come to $23,000. Gerard Coward in corporate accounting sees this additional outlay in wages would be offset by increases in business and thereby ensures we meet our quarterly food sales numbers.

Return on Investment
An increase of staff at Uptown Jazz Cafe is essential to maintaining our existing customer base and increasing it in the future. This increase in staff would guarantee our continued reputation of quality service and quality food. If possible, please respond with your thoughts on this proposal as soon as possible. I am eager to move forward. If you have any questions, please contact anytime.

Figure: 4.3 Sample   Justification Memo

Legend

1. Memo title at the top margin default.
2. 1 line space between the memo title and the header information.
3. 1 line space between the header info and the subject line.
4. 1 line space between the subject line and the first sub-heading.
5. All paragraphs should be single spaced.
6. 1 line space between all single spaced paragraphs.
7. 1 line space between all content areas.
8. 1 line space between bullets and 'costs' area.
9. 1 line space

MEMORANDUM

To: Jim Myers, President, Uptown Jazz Café, Inc.
From: Bill Wyatt, Manager, Uptown Jazz Café, Houston,
Date: February 11, April 18, 2013

Subject: **Need to Increase Wait Staff**

Background and Recommendation
Our Houston store, Uptown Jazz Café, Beacon Street is not meeting its
3rd quarter projections. Having only 12 wait staff, service to our patrons
has suffered. As a result, our business has shrunk by 30%.

To increase business as well as meet our quarterly sales goals, I recommend that we
hire four additional servers, two additional cooks, and one additional dishwasher.
Additional staff will be able to meet our needs on three fronts: service, food quality,
and sanitation.

Benefits and Costs
Seven full-time staff will have a positive effect on our business.

- Dirty plates, glassware, and eating utensils will not pile up. Tables will be
  bused faster.
- Staff will not be called on to work additional hours and will cut down on
  overtime and work fatigue.
- Waiting time to seat patrons will be decreased.
- Attention to customers will be increased.
- Food to table wait time will be decreased.
- Food Quality will be improved with a greater number of cooks to share
  the order load.

Costs: Initial projections for wages would come to $23,000. Gerard Coward
in corporate accounting sees this additional outlay in wages would be offset
by increases in business and thereby ensures we meet our quarterly food sales
numbers.

Return on Investment
An increase of staff at Uptown Jazz Cafe is essential to maintaining our existing customer base and increasing it in the future. This increase in staff would guarantee our
continued reputation of quality service and quality food. If possible, please respond
with your thoughts on this proposal as soon as possible. I am eager to move forward.
If you have any questions, please contact anytime.

Figure: 4.4   Justification Memo with Spacing Guidelines

Legend

1. Backing. The backing supports the warrants by focusing on the necessity to hire additional personnel because of the loss in business.
2. Claim. The claim makes a clear recommendation for the solution of hiring additional personnel to increase business.
3. Data/Support. Explains specific reasons for a change in hiring policy.
4. Rebuttal. The counter argument would be addressing the costs. That is, is the price tag too large. This rebuttal disables the counter argument by demonstrating how the cost would be offset. In other words, the new staff would not put a burden on the budget.
5. Warrants. Information that addresses the boss's concern that hiring additional staff may or may not ensure growth in revenue.

MEMORANDUM

To: Jim Myers, President, Uptown Jazz Café, Inc.
From: Bill Wyatt, Manager, Uptown Jazz Café, Houston,
Date: February 11, April 18, 2013

Subject: **Need to Increase Wait Staff**

Background and Recommendation

Our Houston store, Uptown Jazz Café, Beacon Street is not meeting its 3rd quarter projections. Having only 12 wait staff, service to our patrons has suffered. As a result, our business has shrunk by 30%.

To increase business as well as meet our quarterly sales goals, I recommend that we hire four additional servers, two additional cooks, and one additional dishwasher. Additional staff will be able to meet our needs on three fronts: service, food quality, and sanitation.

Benefits and Costs

Seven full-time staff will have a positive effect on our business.

- Dirty plates, glassware, and eating utensils will not pile up. Tables will be bused much faster.
- Staff will not be called on to work additional hours and will cut down on overtime and work fatigue.
- Waiting time to seat patrons will be decreased.
- Attention to customers will be increased.
- Food to table wait time will be decreased.
- Food Quality will be improved with a greater number of cooks to share the order load.

Costs: Initial projections for wages would come to $23,000. Gerard Coward in corporate accounting sees this additional outlay in wages would be offset by increases in business and thereby ensures we meet our quarterly food sales numbers.

Return on Investment

An increase of staff at Uptown Jazz Cafe is essential to maintaining our existing customer base and increasing it in the future. This increase in staff would guarantee our continued reputation of quality service and quality food. If possible, please respond with your thoughts on this proposal as soon as possible. I am eager to move forward. If you have any questions, please contact anytime.

Figure: 4.5   Toulmin version showing placement and explanation of Toulmin elements.

THE RECAP MEMO

When Do You Write a Recap Memo?

The Occasion arises when there has been a meeting or event that requires a written record of discussed topics, plans of action, and/or future projections.

What's the PMB?

The Purpose A recap memo recaps meetings or events. It is distributed to the people who were in attendance. This memo goes further than a simple restating of past events and discussions. Yes, it is informational, but it also puts forth a subtle argument somewhat different from what you would expect.

Generally, arguments in business writing seek to change things or to get people to switch positions. The purpose of a persuasive recap memo is to persuade the audience of ultimate success while at the same time imparting information. Remember, when it comes to these types of memos, it is not enough just to pass on information of what has been. You must give the information purpose as well. Its purpose *will be to project achievement.*

The Message Because this memo is persuasive, the opening paragraph should clearly state a claim or proposition. This proposition should reference the purpose for the meeting/discussion and project a successful outcome. The events that actually took place will have to be detailed in the body paragraph. These details will serve as support for your proposed success. Be sure to capture the information that best points to this. This assumes a thoughtful and productive meeting. You will want credible information that implies achievement.

The closing paragraph will contain your warrants. It will further instill the idea of a winning outcome by addressing the unstated beliefs of the audience. Remember, the purpose of this type of persuasive recap is to provide information and to convince your audience that success is on the horizon.

The Benefit The benefit of writing a persuasive recap memo with an argumentative model is creating confidence and promoting success among your bosses and colleagues. With this type of memo, you can create an image that projects competence and optimism. High level executives, managers, and supervisors always want to believe maximum achievement is possible.

Two Examples of a Recap Memo to follow:

- An unmarked version for study
- A marked version to study the placement of Toulmin elements and focus on the argument in the document

MEMORANDUM

To: Jerry Stillwell, VP of Instruction
From: Patricia Miller, Associate Dean, Writing and Communications
Date: March 6, 20XX

Subject: **Course Alignment Task Force**

Per our conversation on the course alignment task force, we have conducted
our first meeting outlining the objectives of the task force. Based on our initial
discussions, we are confident we will be able to access preparedness of English
composition students after having completed development writing and the writing
component in the English for
speakers of other languages.

Our committee consists of one instructor from each of the departments in the
study: English, developmental writing, and ESOL. Each representative instructor
explained the design of the their first level course and expected student learning
outcomes. Based on this information, we created a diagram that illustrated points
at which students are required to pass exit exams before moving forward from
ESOL to developmental.

We have determined that it will be necessary to look at the exit exam content and
student performance as the next step in our process. We will be working closely
with the testing center for past exit scores and the research department for grade
distribution in each of the three courses. Ultimately, we will be able to definitively
point out the weak areas in the exit exam process and improve student performance
in credit English composition classes.

Rest assured, we are committed to this project and look forward to its
successful completion.

cc: Ralph Smith, Dean of Academic Development
    Grace Stevens, Dean of ESOL

Figure: 4.6 Sample   Recap Memo

Legend

1. Claim or proposition – This claim instills confidence that there will be a successful outcome.
2. Recap of events. Support – This area convinces the reader that a successful outcome is forthcoming giving the caliber of the committee members and the work they were able to accomplish so quickly.
3. Additional Support
4. *This sentence is considered a closing but it also address audience Warrants. In this case, the audience is the VP. The writer assumes the VP believes in and desires a successful outcome for the study. Therefore, the writer reinforces this belief.*

MEMORANDUM

To: Jerry Stillwell, VP of Instruction
From: Patricia Miller, Associate Dean, Writing and Communications
Date: March 6, 20XX

Subject: **Course Alignment Task Force**

1 — Per our conversation on the course alignment task force, we have conducted our first meeting outlining the objectives of the task force. Based
on our initial discussions, we are confident we will be able to access
preparedness of English composition students after having completed
development writing and the writing component in the English for
speakers of other languages.

2 — Our committee consists of one instructor from each of the departments
in the study: English, developmental writing, and ESOL. Each representative instructor explained the design of the their first level course
and expected student learning outcomes. Based on this information, we
created a diagram that illustrated points at which students are required to
pass exit exams before moving forward from ESOL to developmental.

3 — We have determined that it will be necessary to look at the exit exam
content and student performance as the next step in our process. We will
be working closely with the testing center for past exit scores and the
research department for grade distribution in each of the three courses.
Ultimately, we will be able to definitively point out the weak areas in the
exit exam process and improve student performance in credit English
composition classes.

4 — Rest assured, we are committed to this project and look forward to its
successful completion.

cc: Ralph Smith, Dean of Academic Development
    Grace Stevens, Dean of ESOL

Figure: 4.7   Toulmin version showing positioning and explanation of Toulmin elements.

INFORMATIONAL AND PERSUASIVE EMAIL - 4 IMPORTANT FACTORS

As you already know, email, texting, and instant messaging are the most popular forms of communication nowadays. In the office you will use email as your chief form of communication, instant messaging will be next on the list.

For now, let's talk about email. You probably think you know all you need to know. Just fill in the header information and write away. Yes and no. Email is, can, and should be persuasive. You can control the results if you understand the subtle nuances of email. Meaning, you can control the results if you use Toulmin because Toulmin enables you to be convincing. And as I said in the Toulmin section, you are always selling something, or convincing somebody. Here's how it works.

▶ Tone

Email in the workplace needs to be professionally written. You should follow the same rules and guidelines that are laid out in the tone section. They apply all business writing. It's easy to forget when we email because you probably spend more time in personal email than office email. You can create a habit that is hard to break. So forget about how you write in your personal email or texts or instant messages. Do not use text-spelling like 'u' instead of 'you, or 'ur' and 'your. Do not use short-cut abbreviations such as: LOL or BTW or OMG. Keep your tone semi-formal or formal depending on your audience.

▶ Subject Line

Compose an attention-getting subject line. Mangers, supervisors, team members, associates, and technicians, everyone on the job is busy! Everyone is inundated with email nowadays. You must ensure your message gets opened. Do not compose drab, uninteresting, boring subject lines. Yes, keep tone in mind. You must be professional, but you can also use language that produces a sense of urgency. You can use language that implies your message having great value.

➤ Permanence and Accessibility

Never think the recipient[s] of your email will be the only one. NEVER. If you notice, email can be forwarded and copied and redistributed to a variety of audiences. Always assume your email is permanent and accessible by anyone at anytime. You ultimately have no control over your email once you hit the 'send' button.

➤ Persuasive or Informational

Your email messages can either be PERSUASIVE or INFORMATIONAL. You will have to make the decision based on what you are trying to accomplish. Your recipient will see what you want them to see. Email does not have to be purely informational, the message can be persuasive as well. Remember, you are always persuading and convincing someone in the office. How? You frame the Toulmin elements into the body. Even if you're just talking about a new product brochure for the sales department, you can speak of it in such a way as to prove its viability, it's new improvements, or even something as simple as the announcing the benefits of a new design. There are two examples of email explained in this section, INFORMATIONAL and PERSUASIVE. An informational email is different from a persuasive email. INFOMATIONAL EMAIL merely imparts information, much like an announcement. PERSUASIVE EMAIL lays out an argument to convince your reader of necessary or recommended changes you would like to see implemented.

NOTES

GUIDELINES when Writing and Sending Email

- Create an attention-getting, relevant 'Subject Line,' otherwise, your reader may not open it. Make sure the subject line is provocative, establishes a sense of urgency, and implies value. Use words like urgent, follow-up needed, critical.
- Write your email with the full knowledge that unintended audiences may read it.
- Never write suggestive material in an email that your Mother would not be comfortable reading.
- Remember that email is not a wall to hide behind. When you do not have to face your recipient, it is easy to think you can get away things you might otherwise never say if you were toe to toe with your recipient. Sooner or later, you MAY COME FACE TO FACE with him.
- Image – Be polite and professional, do not be combative, sarcastic, or egotistic.
- Never forward messages without the writer's permission.
- Maintain confidentiality – Do not include information in your email that is critical of someone, or complains about co workers and supervisors. Do not include personal information of any kind. Keep your private thoughts and conversations private.
- Do not use workplace email for personal business.

Format

- Keep it short – Email is designed for brief messages. Try to keep to three paragraphs.
- Do not indent paragraphs
- Subject Line – Keep it clear, short, easy to understand
- Signature Block – Always end your message with a formal signature block. You can include a salutation such as: Best, then your name, 'John', but always end with the formal signature block that contains contact information
- Proofread – Always proofread for misspelled words
- Single-Space entire document.
- Avoid tables and bullet points in the body to conserve space.

Legend

1. Header
2. Date
3. Opening paragraph addresses the point of the email and contains the claim.
4. Body paragraphs contain support
5. Closing contains warrants
6. Signature block

BASIC PARTS OF AN EMAIL

①
From: jbarton@topcastind.com
To: 8accountexecs@topcastind.com
Cc: rwilliams@topcastind.com

Date: January 23, 2013 —②

Subject: **New! Revenue Producing Product Brochure**

③ I am pleased to announce the distribution of the new product sales brochure. All account executives will be receiving a 200 count supply by month end. This new brochure will undoubtedly contribute to the success of our company.

④ The newly designed logo is slick, technical and eye-catching. The brochure itself is simplistic in design, yet captures the true sprit of our product. Its viability is assured due to newly written copy that compares and contrasts our product to our competitor's version. It also creates an advantage aesthetically. Its new look represents the most cutting edge practices in visual design.

⑤ I look forward to hearing your comments. The product marketing team understands the challenges with sales and promotional materials you face in this competitive market. We have also addressed your concerns for market research. This new product brochure is the result of that research. It is the first of many new sales materials that are in development.

Best,

⑥
John Barton
Director, Marketing
Top-Cast Industries, Inc.
Phone: 333-664-8972
Fax: 333-664-8999

Legend - INFORMATIONAL EMAIL

1. **Announcement** – Your subject line is a brief announcement of the new information you will provide. This section offers a benefit for your announcement.
2. **Details** – Notes explaining your announcement.
3. **Conclusion** – A brief statement of any benefits that will result from the new information you are providing.

INFORMATIONAL EMAIL - EXAMPLE

From: jbarton@topcastind.com
To: 8accountexecs@topcastind.com
Cc: rwilliams@topcastind.com

Subject: New Product Brochure

Date: January 23, 2013

① I am pleased to announce the distribution of the new product sales brochure. All account executives will be receiving a 200 count supply by month end. *This new brochure will undoubtedly contribute to the success of our company.*

② *The newly designed logo is slick, technical and eye-catching. The brochure itself is simplistic in design, yet captures the true sprit of our product. Its viability is assured due to newly written copy that compares and contrasts our product to our competitor's version. It also creates an advantage aesthetically. Its new look represents the most cutting edge practices in visual design.*

③ I look forward to hearing your comments. *The product marketing team understands the challenges you face in this competitive market. Particularly those that deal with sales and promotional materials. We have also addressed your concerns for market research. This new product brochure is the result of that research.* It is the first of many new sales materials that are in development.

Best,

John Barton
Director, Marketing
Top-Cast Industries, Inc.

This is a simple informational email that announces or presents new information. It includes 3 areas of discussion: Announcement, Details, Conclusion.

PERSUASIVE EMAIL— (3) EXAMPLES BASED ON THE FOLLOWING SCENARIO

- Read Only Version
- Toulmin Version
- Improper Tone Version

SCENARIO:

Two divisions of the same company operate under different brands. Jane, the manager of one division is coordinating a customer event that will include customers from both divisions of the company. Jane sent an e-mail to the manager of the other division requesting that the event invitations be branded with the brand of Jane's division, even though it was for clients of both divisions. Lisa, the other manager responded with the following e-mail.

From: Lisa Smith, Treasury Services Division
To: Jane Reynolds, Wealth Mgmt Division
cc: Carl Alton, Vice-President Event Management

Date: April 17, 2013

Subject: **Maintaining Brand Consistency**

Hi Jane,

Thanks so much for including our division customers in your event. This type of collaboration will certainly help drive company business.

One important focus for my division is brand consistency in our customer communications. My concern with your proposed approach is that our clients know us as Treasury Services. Receiving an invitation from Wealth Management division would be confusing at best.

I worry that overall event attendance may suffer since treasury services customers may not understand the collaboration. I fear that the absence of focus on our division would impact the meeting schedule. With respect, I also question the overall objective of the event. To my understanding, it should be a joint venture equal in all respects. Why not revisit the subject which will likely impact the design of the invitation.

Keeping our customers and the welfare of the bank in mind, I would like to propose that we use both brands on the invitation as a start and revisit the objective of the event and plan accordingly. All together, this should remove any question in the minds of the attendees as to who is extending the invitation. This will also help to paint a picture of the size and strength of our bank which should ultimately improve business.

Let me know what you think.

Lisa Smith
Manager, Treasury Services Division
Big Bank, Inc.
749-555-0000
LSmith@bigbank.com

Figure: 4.8 Persuasive Email   This email is a read only version.

Legend

1. Always open with a congenial statement to break the ice in a friendly way.
2. **Claim** – Your claim is the item that you are most concerned about, you want to ensure clients know your group as Treasury Services
3. **Support** – You want to convince your supervisor that your concern is legitimate. These are the reasons.
4. **Warrants** – This information addresses concerns of your supervisor who would worry that attendees would be confused over which group is extending the invitation. It also addresses an unstated belief that your supervisor wants bank business to improve.
5. Signature Block

From: Lisa Smith, Treasury Services Division
To: Jane Reynolds, Wealth Mgmt Division
cc: Carl Alton, Vice-President Event Management

Date: April 17, 2013

Subject: **Maintaining Brand Consistency**

Hi Jane,

(1) Thanks so much for including our division customers in your event. This type of collaboration will certainly help drive company business.

(2) One important focus for my division is brand consistency in our customer communications. My concern with your proposed approach is that our clients know us as Treasury Services. Receiving an invitation from Wealth Management division would be confusing at best.

(3) I worry that overall event attendance may suffer since treasury services customers may not understand the collaboration. I fear that the absence of focus on our division would impact the meeting schedule. With respect, I also question the overall objective of the event. To my understanding, it should be a joint venture equal in all respects. Why not revisit the subject which will likely impact the design of the invitation.

(4) Keeping our customers and the welfare of the bank in mind, I would like to propose that we use both brands on the invitation as a start and revisit the objective of the event and plan accordingly. All together, this should remove any question in the minds of the attendees as to who is extending the invitation. This will also help to paint a picture of the size and strength of our bank which should ultimately improve business.

Let me know what you think.

(5) Lisa Smith
Manager, Treasury Services Division
Big Bank, Inc.
749-555-0000
LSmith@bigbank.com

Figure: 4.9 Persuasive Email–Toulmin   This email contains the minimum three elements: claim, support, and warrants.

Legend

1. Entire email contains slang, contractions and text language. (*See words in bold italics*)

From: Lisa Smith, Treasury Services Division
To: Jane Reynolds, Wealth Mgmt Division
cc: Carl Alton, Vice-President Event Management

Date: April 17, 2013

Subject: **Maintaining Brand Consistency**

Hi Jane,

What's up! Can't believe *u* got on board with including our division customers in your event. *It's about time we teamed up for the big show. It'll look like we've got each other's back.* And this is good for business, *know what I sayin?*

I really want our customers to be able to tell us apart. *I mean, be able to know for sure that they are at the right event. What's got me going* about your plan is that our customers know us as Treasury Services and if they receive an invitation from Wealth Management they will be confused.

I think event attendance will suffer and I fear *we're gonna come out on the loosin end. Plus, I don't even understand the whole point of your event. What's the 411? Bring me into focus...*it's pretty hazy in here....*LOL.*

Hopefully I can come to some decision on the brand names for our groups. *I hope you're down with this, okay?* Remember, it is about retaining and growing business.

Waiting for *ur* reply. I need to know if *u r* with me on this.

Lisa Smith
Manager, Treasury Services Division
Big Bank, Inc.
749-555-0000
LSmith@bigbank.com

Figure: 4.10 Persuasive Email with Improper Tone   This type of email is inappropriate for the workplace. See examples of informal tone and slang language in ***bold italic***

EXERCISES

1. You have been elected Student Government President. There are changes you would like to see take place on campus. It could be things like smoke-free environments, recycling, better security measures, or more computer labs. Write a **standard memo** to the college President in which you outline and argue the validity of the proposed changes.

2. If you are currently working at a job, think of a process you would like to see improved or a problem that needs to be solved in order to increase business or improve service. Write a **justification memo** persuading your manager to implement your proposal.

3. You are either a college student or employed in an office. Pick **one** of the two options and write a **persuasive email**.

   • Choose a subject with which you are very familiar at work. Write a persuasive email to your supervisor in which you take a position and propose changes to the status quo.

   • Choose a subject with which you are very familiar at school. Write a persuasive email to the Dean of Student Affairs in which you take a position and propose changes to the status quo.

Image © ARTZSAMUI, 2013. Used under license from Shutterstock, Inc.

CLOSING THE DEAL

WRITING PERSUASIVE LETTERS

OVERVIEW

This section will focus on persuasive workplace letters. It is divided into four areas of content and illustrations: a brief review of the Toulmin Elements of argumentation, standard parts of a letter, letter formats, and ten useful examples of workplace letters.

Have you heard the old saying, 'there's a time and a place for everything?' This applies to workplace letters, email, and memos. In this case, let's talk about letters. There is a particular 'time and place' for letters.

A letter may be composed for colleagues within your company. A letter may be composed for clients or customers outside your company. Letters may be composed to gather information or show appreciation. They can solicit new business or convey bad news. They can announce promotions or terminate employment. In short, letters have an inherent amount of power that sets them apart from email and memos.

This power is persuasion. A letter is designed to convince its reader, to affect the motion of ideas, in other words, to change minds. And is must do this within the confines of one page. When you read the word persuasion, argument should come to mind. When argument comes to mind, you should think about Toulmin once again. Toulmin is the power of persuasion and Toulmin is the framework with which you should compose persuasive workplace letters.

Persuasive workplace letters that use the Toulmin Model of Argumentation should have three characteristics:

Purpose A desired effect, a goal or intended outcome

Message Persuasive communication using the Toulmin model

Benefit Something that will be gained, profited, advanced, or promoted.

In this section, we will refer to these characteristics as PMB. All persuasive letters will have PMB, *a purpose, a convincing message, and a worthwhile benefit.*

This section will focus on ten useful types of workplace letters that can be used within the company or outside the company. They are all designed to be persuasive using elements from the Toulmin Model of Argumentation.

- Inquiry Letter
- Sales Letter
- Bad News Adjustment Letter
- Good News Adjustment Letter
- Appreciation Letter
- Additional Duties Letter
- Complaint Letter
- Arguable Claim Letter
- Reprimand Letter for Poor Performance
- Reprimand Letter for Tardiness

Each letter will have its own *PMB* page as explanation. Each letter will be presented in three formats: a read-only version, a version with highlighted Toulmin Elements, and a formatted version showing spacing requirements. Before we study the 10 useful letters, we will need to review Toulmin, the basic parts of a letter, and study the basic formats of business letters.

THE SIX ELEMENTS OF TOULMIN

The Six Elements of the Toulmin Model of Argumentation

These elements should be present in any business communication designed to persuade. Before you study these elements, review your reading assignments in the textbook. You will be asked to create a graded assignment [memo] to demonstrate your understanding of persuasion in business communication. The assignment is at the end of this document.

- **The Claim:** *This is the proposition in any business document. This will be what the document wants you to buy, believe, or do.*
- **The Support/Data:** *This will be the evidence that will persuade you to accept the claim. Things like opinions, reasons, examples, facts, data, information, and statistics.*
- **The Warrants:** *Warrants are very interesting and very important to the art of persuasion. They are intangibles for the most part. These are things that your audience believes about certain issues. The easiest way to describe them is to call them assumptions, widely held values, commonly accepted beliefs, cultural values, and generally accepted truths. Always remember that your audience will carry these things internally and they will drive his or her ability to accept what you are proposing.*
- **The Backing:** *Backing is a strategy that supports the warrants of your audience to your advantage. They go hand in hand. This would be information included in your document that speaks to your audiences' basic beliefs, values, commonly held truths about specific issues. You would include this information in your business document only if you have a strong sense of your audiences' warrants.*
- **The Rebuttal:** *Exposing anticipated counter-arguments or possible weaknesses in your proposal, letter, or other business communication is called a rebuttal. If you are countering an anticipated argument, include information to refute it. If you are addressing your argument's possible weaknesses, shore them up. 'A good defense is sometimes a good offense'.*
- **The Qualifier:** *Qualifiers are words or language that will not pin you down to a certainty. Remember, there are no guarantees in the business world, thus no guarantee that your proposal, report, or letter will absolutely 'change the world.' Do not use words in your document like 'always' 'absolutely' 'never.' Use words like maybe, sometimes, might, could, probably, or possibly.*

THE 6 STANDARD PARTS OF A LETTER

1. The Date All letters must have a date. Depending on the letter format, the date can either be against the left margin in a block format, or aligned at the center in a modified-block format. It must be spelled out in a traditional form ONLY. The date is generally situated at the top margin default if there is no company letterhead or 5 – 9 line spaces below company letter head.

For example: October 12, 1986

DO NOT USE a numbered format such as 12.15.86 or 12/15/86

2. The Inside Address The inside address will be positioned below the date line. The exact line spacing between the date line and the inside address will depend on the style and length of the letter.

Mr. John Smith
ABC Electronics
2312 Carrollton Lane
Pine Bluff, AR 45362

3. The Salutation The salutation is located one line space below the inside address. It must include a specific name and end with a colon. Do not use a comma.

Dear Mr. Smith:
Dear Ms. Smith:
Dear Professor Martin:
Dear Dr. Smith:

4. The Body The body must begin 2 line spaces below the salutation or attention line. All of the paragraphs should be single spaced. There should be one line space between each body paragraph. Keep your body concise. You must keep the letter to one page only.

5. The Complimentary Closing The closing should be two line spaces below the last body paragraph. The type of closing you use depends on the type of relationship you have with the reader. Typically, the more removed you are from the reader, the more formal the closing.

Use customary closings that do not display emotion.

- Sincerely,
- Regards,

Other types of closings include the following:

- Best, [informal business tone]
- Respectfully, [used with elected officials]

NOT used in workplace letters

- Yours truly,
- Sincerely yours,
- Best Wishes,

6. The Printed Signature Your name and title should be four line spaces below the closing. This is sometimes called a signature block when it includes the closing.

Sincerely,

Jan Smith
Sales Manager

When including a company name, type in FULL CAPS if the letter is representing a group and not an individual. It should be two line spaces below the closing. Then type your printed name and title in four line spaces below the company name.

Regards,

MASON TECHNOLOGIES INC.

Jan Smith
Sales Manger

Optional Parts include the following:

An Attention Line Used when you have no specific person for a salutation
ATTENTION: Human Resources Department

A Subject Line Used with memos but can be used in a business letter with a salutation if the reader has no expectation of the letter. The subject line should be placed above the salutation.

SUBJECT: 3rd Quarter Sales Figures

An Enclosure Notation This notation should be one line space below the printed signature line if there are enclosed documents.

Enclosure
Enclosures 2

Copy Notation This notation designates people who receive copies of the letter. It should be one line space below the previous line.

cc: John Smith

Legend

1. Company Logo
2. Date
3. Inside Address
4. Salutation
5. Single Spaced Body Paragraphs
6. Closing
7. Printed Signature, title and Company
8. Enclosure notation
9. Courtesy Copy notation.

Davis Climate Systems, Inc —(1)

December 12, 2013 —(2)

(3)— Mr. Stanley Mackey
Global Account Manager
Overnight Freight Forwarders, Inc.
Maryville, TN 31209

Dear Mr. Smith: —(4)

I am writing to you because Overnight Freight Forwarders is one of the leaders in international shipping which comes as no news to you. I am sure you wish to grow your business as we wish to grow ours here at Davis Climate Systems.

My company has just signed a contract with an Italian automaker to ship five - hundred auto air condition compressors per month to various factory locations in Europe. I am in the process of selecting an international freight forwarder and I am interested in hiring your company. Davis Climate Systems will be very good for Overnight Forwarders, but first we would need some basic information.

(5)— Would you be able to put together a proposal that would include volume dis-counted shipping rates, forwarding fees, and expedited transit times? All shipments will originate in Dallas, TX and be shipped to Frankfurt, Germany, Amsterdam, Netherlands, and Rome, Italy. Why will Davis Climate be good for your company?

Given the nature of our product, frequency of shipments, and destinations, a ship-ping contract of this caliber will be very lucrative. I dare say we will be one of your 'A' accounts. You would be our only freight forwarder. There are plans to increase shipments by 10% every quarter.

Clearly, this is a win-win situation for both our companies. I look forward to hearing from you. Because I will need to make a decision by March 31, I would greatly appre-ciate receiving your proposal before this date. Should you need additional informa-tion, you can reach me at my office, 800-356-8754.

(6)— Sincerely,

(7)— Jack Rossi, Logistics Manager
Davis Climate Systems, Inc.

Enclosure 2 —(8)

(9)— cc: Lewis Reynolds

Figure: 5.1 Parts of a Letter - Block Style

March 17, 2012

Mr. Rufus Randall, Distribution Supervisor
Business Interiors Inc.
1234 Plaza Dr.
San Diego, CA 94336

Dear Mr. Randall:

As you have been aware, our warehouse facility has been expanding its services for the benefit of our clients. Recently, the board of directors appropriated additional budget dollars to aid in this expansion. This is an investment in the future of our company that will grow profitability.

With this, we would like to inform you that we are giving you the opportunity to take part. Your current position of Distribution Manager will be expanded to Logistics Manager. Because the company is expanding its global business, our transportation needs will include international shipping.

We feel that your experience in import/export documentation, import administration, air freight, railroad, and overseas container shipping will be beneficial to this new position. Additionally, your past performance as Distribution Manger has consistently exceeded expectations. Apart from the additional duties this new position will require, you will be allowed flexible hours and an increase in compensation to be discussed at a later date.

While this is another bold step for our company, we feel that this would also help us gather more attention and recognition on the world stage. Being a part of this would be a great contribution. This should be an exciting experience for you. We hope that you will accept this new position.

Sincerely,

David Morris, Director
Human Resources

cc: Tom Rawlins, Vice-President Operations

Figure: 5.2 Typical Letter in Block Style

FORMATTING GUIDELINES

1. The date line begins at the top margin default which should be the 1-inch mark on the ruler.
2. There should be 4 – 6-line spaces between the date line and the inside address.
3. There should be 1-line space between the inside address and the salutation.
4. There should be 1-line space between the salutation and the first body paragraph.
5. There should be 1-line space between each single-spaced body paragraph.
6. There should be 1-line space between the last body paragraph and the closing.
7. There should be 4-line space between the closing and the printed signature.
8. There should be 1-line space between the printed signature and any additional notifications such as an enclosure line, courtesy copy line [s], resume line.

Legend

1. Return address begins at 1 inch top margin default. It is centered in the document given the left and right margins. Each line should be left-justified.
2. 4 – 6 line spaces between the return address and the inside address depending on length.
3. 1 line space between the inside address and the salutation.
4. 1 line space between the salutation and the first body paragraph.
5. 1 line space between each single spaced body paragraph.
6. Body paragraphs should be single spaced.
7. 1 line space between the last paragraph and the signature block.
8. The return address and the signature block should be centered horizontally, and aligned on the left.

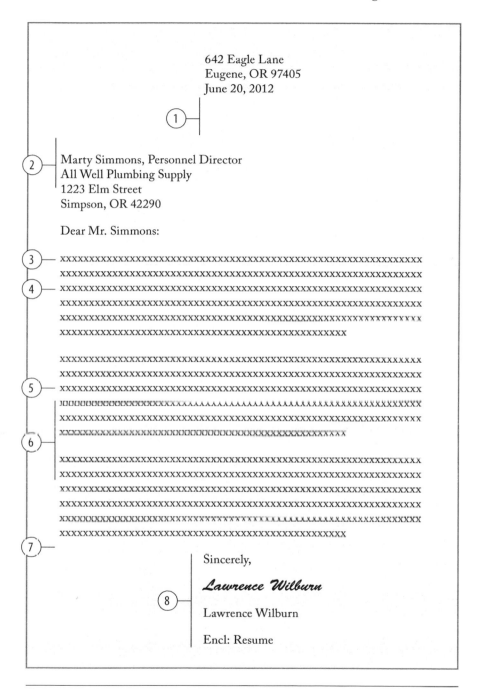

Figure: 5.3 Spacing Guide for a Typical Letter in Modified-Block Style

THE ADDITIONAL DUTIES LETTER

When Do You Write an Additional Duties Letter?

The Occasion arises when an employee is offered one of the following prospects:

- An opportunity for promotion or raise in salary
- An opportunity to showcase skills and abilities
- An opportunity to take on additional responsibilities altruistically

What's the PMB?

The Purpose An additional duties letter can be a good thing or a bad thing. Normally, people are given additional duties because their level of work is very good. There may even be a promotion in the works. Hence, the additional duties could somewhat of a test. Or, it could absolutely be the precursor to a formal promotion. This is generally the case. However, some additional duties letters merely add work or responsibility to the employee's current work load without any particular compensation.

The Message The letter should be formal in tone and include high points in the employee's past performance. Because all business writing is 'persuading' or convincing', Toulmin elements should be included. There should be a clear proposition put forth [claim] that states the employee will be given additional duties. Support should be present which justifies the additional duties. Warrants should be present which will address the employee's possible desire to be promoted. Lastly, there should be a rebuttal which will address a possible counter argument from an employee that may not wish to have additional duties. Note the positioning of the Toulmin elements in the sample letter.

The Benefit What is the benefit of writing a letter of this type? You may receive an apology, some sort of restitution, have unpleasant circumstances made better, or have unfair treatment documented.

Three Examples of an Additional Duties Letter to follow:

- An unmarked version for study
- A marked version to study the placement of Toulmin elements and focus on the argument in the document.
- A formatted version that shows the correct spacing between content areas in the letter.

March 17, 2012

Mr. Rufus Randall
Business Interiors Inc.
Distribution Department

Dear Mr. Randall:

As you have been aware, our warehouse facility has been expanding its services for the benefit of our clients. Recently, the board of directors appropriated additional budget dollars to aid in this expansion. This is an investment in the future of our company that will grow profitability.

With this, we would like to inform you that we are giving you the opportunity to take part. Your current position of Distribution Manager will be expanded to Logistics Manager. Because the company is expanding its global business, our transportation needs will include international shipping.

We feel that your experience in import/export documentation, import administration, air freight, railroad, and overseas container shipping will be beneficial to this new position. Additionally, your past performance as Distribution Manger has consistently exceeded expectations. Apart from the additional duties this new position will require, you will be allowed flexible hours and an increase in compensation to be discussed at a later date.

While this is another bold step for our company, we feel that this would also help us gather more attention and recognition on the world stage. Your being a part of this would be a great contribution. This should be an exciting experience for you. We hope that you will accept this new position.

Sincerely,

David Morris

David Morris, Director
Human Resources

cc: Tom Rawlins, Vice-President Operations

Figure: 5.4 Read-Only Version Additional Duties Letter

Legend

1. Date – Begins at the 1 inch default for top margin.
2. 5 – 12 line spaces between the date line and the inside address. Depending upon the length and style of the letter.
3. 1 line space between the inside address and the salutation.
4. 1 line space between the salutation and the first paragraph.
5. 1 line space between all single spaced body paragraphs.
6. 1 line space between the last body paragraph and the closing.
7. 4 line spaces between the closing and the printed signature.
8. 1 line space between the printed signature and the CC line.

March 17, 2012 —①

②

Mr. Rufus Randall
Business Interiors Inc.
Distribution Department

③

Dear Mr. Randall:

④

As you have been aware, our warehouse facility has been expanding its services for the benefit of our clients. Recently, the board of directors appropriated additional budget dollars to aid in this expansion. This is an investment in the future of our company that will grow profitability.

With this, we would like to inform you that we are giving you the opportunity to take part. Your current position of Distribution Manager will be expanded to Logistics Manager. Because the company is expanding its global business, our transportation needs will include international shipping.

⑤

We feel that your experience in import/export documentation, import administration, air freight, railroad, and overseas container shipping will be beneficial to this new position. Additionally, your past performance as Distribution Manger has consistently exceeded expectations. Apart from the additional duties this new position will require, you will be allowed flexible hours and an increase in compensation to be discussed at a later date.

While this is another bold step for our company, we feel that this would also help us gather more attention and recognition on the world stage. Your being a part of this would be a great contribution. This should be an exciting experience for you. We hope that you will accept this new position.

⑥

Sincerely,

⑦

David Morris

David Morris, Director
Human Resources

⑧

cc: Tom Rawlins, Vice-President Operations

Figure: 5.5 Spacing Guide

Legend

1. **Warrants** – This opening paragraph of congeniality assumes that the reader is interested in the company's growth.
2. **Backing** – This sentence backs up the warrant that assumes the employee is interested in the company's future and wants to take part and thus brighten her future as well.
3. *Claim* – This is the proposition being put forth, a claim that Ms. Randall should be given additional duties. The following support will argue this proposition.
4. **Support** – This is the support area which makes the case for an expansion of duties.
5. **Rebuttal** – There may be some resistance which can be viewed as a counter argument from the employee to not accept additional duties. This sentence addresses those concerns.
6. **Warrants** – These are additional warrants that assumes the employee wants a promotion and all of the career benefits it implies.

March 17, 2012

Ms. Barbra Randall
Business Interiors Inc.
Distribution Department

Dear Ms. Randall:

(1) As you have been aware, our warehouse facility has been expanding its services for the benefit of our clients. Recently, the board of directors appropriated additional budget dollars to aid in this expansion. This is an investment in the future of our company that will grow profitability.

(2) With this, we would like to inform you that we are giving you the opportunity to take part. Because the company is expanding its global business, our transportation needs will include international shipping. (3) ***Your current position of Distribution Manager will be expanded to Logistics Manager.***

(4) We feel that your experience in import/export documentation, import administration, air freight, railroad, and overseas container shipping will be beneficial to this new position. Additionally, your past performance as Distribution Manger has consistently exceeded expectations. (5) Apart from the additional duties this new position will require, you will be allowed flexible hours and an increase in compensation to be discussed at a later date.

(6) While this is another bold step for our company, we feel that this would also help us gather more attention and recognition on the world stage. Your being a part of this would be a great contribution. This should be an exciting experience for you. We hope that you will accept this new position.

Sincerely,

David Morris

David Morris, Director
Human Resources

cc: Tom Rawlins, Vice-President Operations

Figure: 5.6 Toulmin Version

THE APPRECIATION LETTER

When Do You Write an Appreciation Letter?

The Occasion arises when an employee or a vendor is offered one of the following prospects:

- An opportunity for a promotion
- An opportunity for more business
- An opportunity to be recognized among his/her peers

What's the PMB?

The Purpose Everyone likes to feel appreciated. Everyone likes to know they are doing a good job. Everyone lines to feel that doing a good job will result in some time of reward. The purpose of an appreciation letter is to do just that, show appreciation. It can also announce a reward of compensation or recognition.

The Message The letter should be formal in tone and should specifically point out 'positives.' Even an appreciation or 'thank you' letter can be an argument, hence it can include Toulmin. Remember, you are convincing someone that they did a nice job. Because all business writing is 'persuading' or convincing,' Toulmin elements should be included. There should be a clear proposition put forth [claim] that states the employee or vendor has been doing an excellent job. Support should present specific examples of a 'great job' being done. Warrants should be present which will address the employee's or the vendor's possible desire to be promoted or rewarded new or continuing business. No rebuttal necessary in an appreciation letter. It would be highly unusual for an employee or vendor to refuse a 'thank you.' The example letter has a 'vendor' as subject. You will not the positioning of the warrants, support, and claim.

The Benefit What is the benefit of writing a letter of this type? You send a clear and positive message that encourages the employee and/or vendor. As in the additional duties letter, you are telling someone that they are doing a great job. They have been noticed and will likely be rewarded in some tangible way.

Three Examples of an Appreciation Letter to follow:
- A Read Only Version version for study
- A marked version to study the placement of Toulmin elements and focus on the argument in the document
- A formatted version that shows the correct spacing between content areas in the letter

February 16, 2012

Mr. Lewis Motley, Owner
Lewis Motley Cadillac
235 Downs Ave.
Chicago, IL 30221

Dear Mr. Motley:

For fifteen years, Royal Limousine Service has purchase all of its vehicles from Lewis Motley Cadillac. During this time, we have exclusively used your service department for routine maintenance and incidental repairs. You have provided quality consistent service.

Our business requires perfectly running vehicles 24 hours a day, 7 days a week. Because of this, excessive downtime for vehicle repairs can make our life difficult. Thanks to your excellent service, we experience no such difficulties. Appointment times are always compatible with our needs. Your service technicians are knowledgeable and prompt when returning calls. The repair turn times are always reasonable and the vehicles clean at pick up.

We understand Motley Cadillac strives to be the best Cadillac dealer in greater downtown Chicago. The level of service you continue to offer will no doubt grow your customer base and ensure loyal clients. We hope to be one of them.

To this end, we would like to cater lunch for the service department employees as soon as possible. Please call me and let me know when we can schedule this event.

Sincerely,

Joshua Stern

Joshua Stern, Owner
Royal Limousine Service

Figure: 5.7 Read-Only Version Appreciation Letter

Legend

1. Dateline at top margin default.
2. 5 – 12 line spaces between the date and the inside address depending upon the length and style of the letter.
3. 1 line space between the inside address and the salutation.
4. 1 line space between salutation and first body paragraph.
5. 1 line space between each single spaced body paragraph.
6. 1 line space between the last paragraph and the closing.
7. 4 line spaces between the closing and the printed signature.

February 16, 2012 —①

②

Mr. Lewis Motley, Owner
Lewis Motley Cadillac
235 Downs Ave.
Chicago, IL 30221

③

Dear Mr. Motley:

④

For fifteen years, Royal Limousine Service has purchase all of its vehicles
from Lewis Motley Cadillac. During this time, we have exclusively used
your service department for routine maintenance and incidental repairs.
You have provided quality consistent service.

Our business requires perfectly running vehicles 24 hours a day, 7 days a
week. Because of this, excessive downtime for vehicle repairs can make
our life difficult. Thanks to your excellent service, we experience no such
difficulties. Appointment times are always compatible with our needs.
Your service technicians are knowledgeable and prompt when returning
calls. The repair turn times are always reasonable and the vehicles clean at
pick up.

⑤

We understand Motley Cadillac strives to be the best Cadillac dealer in
greater downtown Chicago. The level of service you continue to offer will
no doubt grow your customer base and ensure loyal clients. We hope to be
one of them.

To this end, we would like to cater lunch for the service department
employees as soon as possible. Please call me and let me know when we
can schedule this event.

⑥

Sincerely,

⑦ *Joshua Stern*

Joshua Stern, Owner
Royal Limousine Service

Figure: 5.8 Spacing Version

Legend

1. *Claim*
2. **Support** – Facts that support the claim of good service.
3. **Warrants** – This paragraph represents the beliefs in the mind of the dealership owner: He more than likely believes that good consistent service will result in return clients and new business.

February 16, 2012

Mr. Lewis Motley, Owner
Lewis Motley Cadillac
235 Downs Ave.
Chicago, IL 30221

Dear Mr. Motley:

(1) For fifteen years, Royal Limousine Service has purchase all of its vehicles from Lewis Motley Cadillac. During this time, we have exclusively used your service department for routine maintenance and incidental repairs. *You have provided quality consistent service.*

(2) Our business requires perfectly running vehicles 24 hours a day, 7 days a week. Because of this, excessive downtime for vehicle repairs can make our life difficult. Thanks to your excellent service, we experience no such difficulties. Appointment times are always compatible with our needs. Your service technicians are knowledgeable and prompt when returning calls. The repair turn times are always reasonable and the vehicles clean at pick up.

(3) We understand Motley Cadillac strives to be the best Cadillac dealer in greater downtown Chicago. The level of service you continue to offer will no doubt grow your customer base and ensure loyal clients. We hope to be one of them.

To this end, we would like to cater lunch for the service department employees as soon as possible. Please call me and let me know when we can schedule this event.

Sincerely,

Joshua Stern

Joshua Stern, Owner
Royal Limousine Service

Figure: 5.9 Toulmin Version

THE ARGUABLE CLAIM LETTER

When Do You Write an Arguable Claim Letter?

The Occasion arises when levels of service fail, mistakes are made, or promises are not kept.

What's the PMB?

The Purpose The purpose of an arguable claim letter is to receive restitution for unsatisfactory services or products. It can also be used to complain about unfair treatment. Arguable claim letters will more than likely convey unwelcome news. Therefore, it is essential to keep 'reason' in mind. The main purpose here is to receive a refund, an apology, or a replacement.

The Message Always begin with a congenial statement and try to find some common ground where all parties can agree. Most importantly, always include enough detail. Remember, you are arguing for a specific claim. Your argument will mostly rest on the detail you provide as support. Because this is an arguable claim letter, the Toulmin model is obviously the framework within which to compose the letter. Tone is important as well. Keep your message polite and formal. Stick to the point. Do not veer off on a tirade that makes no sense. Keep emotion out of it.

Guidelines:

- Open with a congenial statement both parties can agree on. This is where you address your reader's warrants. You might reference good service in the past. You might include some allusion to future business if the matter is resolved quickly.
- State your claim clearly. This is where you state what product or service you want replaced, adjusted, or rendered.
- Outline your support for your claim. This is the area in which you provide evidence to support your claim. Your reader must have a reason for meeting your requests.
- Conclude the letter by requesting specific action to be taken. This area can include more warrants such as an appeal to continue the vendor-client relationship in the future, and how a successful solution can ensure new clients for your vendor.

The Benefit What is the benefit of writing a letter of this type? You may receive an apology, some sort of restitution, have unpleasant circumstances made better, or have unfair treatment documented.

Three Examples of an Arguable Claim Letter to follow:
- An unmarked version for study
- A marked version to study the placement of Toulmin elements and focus on the argument in the document
- A formatted version that shows the correct spacing between content areas in the letter

---

September 17, 2012

The Honorable Governor Rick Perry
Texas State Capitol Building
1100 Congress Ave.
Austin, TX 78701

Dear Governor Perry:

As the Governor of Texas, you have built your reputation on improving education. As a student, I have counted on improvements to achieve a better education. However, the education budget for 2013 has been twenty percent for all state colleges. This is extremely distressful.

This cut will cause layoffs of faculty members and increase class size. It will also reduce financial aid and special academic programs. The will undoubtedly reduce admissions. I contacted your office August 28th, 2012 and received little explanation for these cuts.

As students we depend on financial aid to be able to attend school. Without the option of financial aid, many students will be forced to drop out of school. Laying off faculty will cause an increase in class size which will affect learning. Additionally, fewer teachers means fewer sponsors for academic clubs and special programs. When you lower the quality of Texas education, you lower the social and professional quality of Texas residents.

I insist you revisit the budget and reconsider your cuts. One possible alternative would be an increase in corporate taxes. Until now, I supported your party and your policies. At this time, I do not. In the future, if there are positive changes to the education budget, I may be able to lend my support again.

I would appreciate a response to this issue within 30 days.

Sincerely,

Carl Miller

Carl Miller
Student, University of Texas, Austin

Figure: 5.10 Read-Only Version Arguable Claim Letter

Legend

1. Date line is one line space below the top margin default.
2. 5 – 12 line spaces between the date and the inside address depending upon the length and style of the letter.
3. 1 line space between the inside address and the salutation.
4. 1 line space between the salutation and the first body paragraph.
5. 1 line space between each single spaced body paragraph.
6. 1 line space between the closing line and the closing.
7. 4 line spaces between the closing and the printed signature.

September 17, 2012 ──①

②

The Honorable Governor Rick Perry
Texas State Capitol Building
1100 Congress Ave.
Austin, TX 78701

③

Dear Governor Perry:

④

As the Governor of Texas, you have built your reputation on improving education. As a student, I have counted on improvements to achieve a better education.
However, the education budget for 2013 has been cut twenty percent for all state
colleges. This is extremely distressful.

This cut will cause layoffs of faculty members and increase class size. It will also
reduce financial aid and special academic programs. The will undoubtedly reduce
admissions. I contacted your office August 28th, 2012 and received little explanation for these cuts.

⑤

As students we depend on financial aid to be able to attend school. Without the
option of financial aid, many students will be forced to drop out of school. Laying
off faculty will cause an increase in class size which will affect learning. Additionally, fewer teachers mean fewer sponsors for academic clubs and special programs.
When you lower the quality of Texas education, you lower the social and professional quality of Texas residents.

I insist you revisit the budget and reconsider your cuts. One possible alternative
would be an increase in corporate taxes. Until now, I supported your party and
your policies. At this time, I do not. In the future, if there are positive changes to
the education budget, I may be able to lend my support again.

I would appreciate a response to this issue within 30 days.

⑥

Respectfully,

⑦ *Carl Miller*

Carl Miller
Student, University of Texas, Austin

Figure: 5.11 Spacing Version

Legend

1. **Warrant** – Establishes early agreement and addresses what the Governor believes about his performance. This is an unstated warrant on his part.
2. **Claim** – The last line in the first paragraph clearly stating cuts in the budget will be harmful.
3. **Support** – The second and third paragraphs present facts that support the claim.
4. **Rebuttal** – These two sentences challenge the argument that cuts have to be made to education.
5. **Backing** – These last sentences back up the initial warrants. They assume the Governor would like to be re-elected. The writer addresses them in a sense that implies he will not support the Governor unless changes are made.

September 17, 2012

The Honorable Governor Rick Perry
Texas State Capitol Building
1100 Congress Ave.
Austin, TX 78701

Dear Governor Perry:

(1) — As the Governor of Texas, you have built your reputation on improving education. As a student, I have counted on improvements to achieve a better education.
However, the education budget for 2013 has been cut twenty percent for all state
(2) — colleges. *This is extremely distressful and harmful to higher education.*

This cut will cause layoffs of faculty members and increase class size. It will also
reduce financial aid and special academic programs. The will undoubtedly reduce
admissions. I contacted your office August 28th, 2012 and received little explanation for these cuts.

(3) —
As students we depend on financial aid to be able to attend school. Without the
option of financial aid, many students will be forced to drop out of school. Laying
off faculty will cause an increase in class size which will affect learning. Additionally, fewer teachers mean fewer sponsors for academic clubs and special programs.
When you lower the quality of Texas education, you lower the social and professional quality of Texas residents.

(4) — I insist you revisit the budget and reconsider your cuts. One possible alternative
would be an increase in corporate taxes. Until now, I supported your party and
(5) — your policies. At this time, I do not. In the future, if there are positive changes to
the education budget, I may be able to lend my support again.

I would appreciate a response to this issue within 30 days.

Respectfully,

Carl Miller

Carl Miller
Student, University of Texas, Austin

Figure: 5.12 Toulmin Version

THE BAD NEWS ADJUSTMENT LETTER

When Do You Write a Bad News Adjustment Letter?

The Occasion You must write a negative response to a claim from a customer.

What's the PMB?

The Purpose The purpose of this letter is to tell the customer you will not be able to fulfill his exact wish. The purpose of this letter is to be clear in your explanation of why you will not be able to fulfill those wishes. At the same time, the purpose of this letter is to maintain his goodwill. You will want to retain future business.

The Message As in the good news adjustment, always begin with a congenial statement and express regret. End on a positive note. Never place blame. And as with good news adjustment letters, you must be convincing. You are making the case to retain business with your company while at the same time, turning the customer down. Strangely, you must convince the customer you are right without being overly accusatory.

Again, Toulmin will be needed. Your claim will be a refusal to make repairs at the company's expense. Your support must be a statement that outlines exactly why. You will need to create a rebuttal. Most customers will assume the manufacturer should accept all expenses. Lastly, warrants must be placed as well. Warrants will address the unstated belief in the mind of the customer that the product is immune to damage. You can also use warrants to make it clear your company values its customers by absorbing a portion of the shipping costs to retain the business. Carefully study the Toulmin sample to follow.

The Benefit What is the benefit of writing a letter of this type? You keep customers even though you are not able to fulfill their exact wishes. By being honest and sticking to policy, you stand for the integrity of the business. You can also establish goodwill by offering some monetary compensation for repeat business. In short, a big benefit is keeping your customer.

Three Examples of a Bad News Adjustment Letter to follow:
- An unmarked version for study
- A marked version to study the placement of Toulmin elements and focus on the argument in the document
- A formatted version that shows the correct spacing between content areas in the letter

March 16, 2012

Mr. Jarod Smith
2311 West Cutler Dr.
Arlington, TX 73210

Dear Mr. Smith:

It is unfortunate that you have experienced service difficulties with your DVD player. At Brighton Electronics, we take great pride in manufacturing durable players.

We are in receipt of your letter. According to your statement, the DVD player accidentally fell to the floor in the midst of a move. After having received your DVD player at our warranty center, we immediately had it inspected. Upon completion of the inspection, we verified the damage was caused by the fall as you stated. Unfortunately, the warranty does not cover repair charges when the failure is not due to manufacturer error. The repairs will need to be made at your expense.

We have estimated the repair costs to be $123.00. This includes Brighton parts and labor which will ensure optimal performance of the product. Because we wish to retain your business, we will return ship the DVD player at no cost.

If you would like us to proceed with the repairs, please call warranty repair at 1-800-325-4556. Again, we are sorry for the inconvenience and look forward to keeping you as a loyal customer.

Sincerely,

Russell Morgan

Russell Morgan, Manger
Product Warranty Services
Brighton Electronics

cc: Lewis Jamison, Quality Assurance

Figure: 5.13 Read-Only Version Bad News Letter

Legend

1. Date line at the top margin default.
2. 5 – 12 line spaces between the date and the inside address depending upon the length and style of letter.
3. 1 line space between inside address and the salutation.
4. 1 line space between the salutation and the first body paragraph.
5. 1 line space between each single spaced body paragraph.
6. 1 line space between the last paragraph and the closing.
7. 4 line spaces between the closing and the printed signature.
8. 1 line space between the signature block and the courtesy copy line.

March 16, 2012   —①

②

Mr. Jarod Smith
2311 West Cutler Dr.
Arlington, TX 73210

③

Dear Mr. Smith:

④

It is unfortunate that you have experienced service difficulties with your DVD player. At Brighton Electronics, we take great pride in manufacturing durable players.

⑤

We are in receipt of your letter. According to your statement, the DVD player accidentally fell to the floor in the midst of a move. After having received your DVD player at our warranty center, we immediately had it inspected. Upon completion of the inspection, we verified the damage was caused by the fall as you stated. Unfortunately, the warranty does not cover repair charges when the failure is not due to manufacturer error. The repairs will need to be made at your expense.

We have estimated the repair costs to be $123.00. This includes Brighton parts and labor which will ensure optimal performance of the product. Because we wish to retain your business, we will return ship the DVD player at no cost.

If you would like us to proceed with the repairs, please call warranty repair at 1-800-325-4556. Again, we are sorry for the inconvenience and look forward to keeping you as a loyal customer.

⑥

Sincerely,

⑦— *Russell Morgan*

Russell Morgan, Manger
Product Warranty Services
Brighton Electronics

⑧

cc: Lewis Jamison, Quality Assurance

Figure: 5.14 Spacing Version

Legend

1. **Warrants** – Addresses the assumption that the customer believed the DVD player to be durable and survive a fall.
2. **Support** – Facts that support the claim that repairs will need to be a the customer's expense.
3. **Rebuttal** – Most customers will want the manufacturer to absorb all expenses. Write in a rebuttal or counter argument that the manufacturer cannot pay repairs by referencing the warranty policy.
4. *Claim*
5. **Warrants** – Additional warrants that assumes the customer would prefer the manufacturer to repair the player.

March 16, 2012

Mr. Jarod Smith
2311 West Cutler Dr.
Arlington, TX 73210

Dear Mr. Smith:

It is unfortunate that you have experienced service difficulties with your
DVD player. At Brighton Electronics, we take great pride in manufacturing durable players.

We are in receipt of your letter. According to your statement, the DVD
player accidentally fell to the floor in the midst of a move. After having
received your DVD player at our warranty center, we immediately had
it inspected. Upon completion of the inspection, we verified the damage
was caused by the fall as you stated. Unfortunately, the warranty does not
cover repair charges when the failure is not due to manufacturer error.
The repairs will need to be made at your expense. —(4)

We have estimated the repair costs to be $123.00. This includes Brighton
parts and labor which will ensure optimal performance of the product.
Because we wish to retain your business, we will return ship the DVD
player at no cost.

If you would like us to proceed with the repairs, please call warranty
repair at 1-800-325-4556. Again, we are sorry for the inconvenience and
look forward to keeping you as a loyal customer.

Sincerely,

Russell Morgan

Russell Morgan, Manger
Product Warranty Services
Brighton Electronics

cc: Lewis Jamison, Quality Assurance

Figure: 5.15 Toulmin Version

THE COMPLAINT LETTER

When Do You Write a Complaint Letter?

The Occasion is much the same as an arguable claim letter. You use this letter to bring attention to defective products or services. You can also use this type of letter as a means to document poor treatment in the office.

What's the PMB?

The Purpose The purpose of a complaint letter is to call attention to a situation that needs to be changed, 'made right,' or eliminated. Complaint letters do not usually set a time line for response or request specific compensation. In short, they document maltreatment, error, or in some cases, call for help in resolving problems.

The Message The message will also be an argument. Remember, you are complaining about a specific incident. Therefore, you must state the incident clearly. This will be your claim or proposition you are trying to prove. You will need strong support that can document errors maltreatment or problems. You will need a rebuttal, or counter argument in which you debunk 'the other side' of the complaint. For example, in the following sample letter, a business is the 'the other side.' The business will no doubt have their side of the argument. You will also need warrants to keep the tone civil and lay the groundwork for a continued relationship. Note the placement of the Toulmin elements in the sample letter.

This letter deals with a product rather than a fellow employee or boss. Still, the argument will be the same. The claim may change. If we are talking about an office situation, you may have a problem with a supervisor who does not give detailed instructions, yet continuously holds you responsible for failed projects. Rather product or colleague, you will need to state your claim, proposition, or point you must prove. You must have strong support to prove it. You must consider the assumptions, beliefs, better known as unstated warrants of your colleague. You must also be prepared to out wit 'the other side' with rebuttals. In short, Toulmin is the heart of this letter much like the arguable claim letter. Study the sample closely.

The Benefit What is the benefit of writing a letter of this type? Like the arguable claim letter. The writer may receive an apology, some sort of restitution, have unpleasant circumstances made better, or have unfair treatment documented. Bottom line, complaint letters DOCUMENT things; they create records of activities, mishaps, interactions. Without records or documentation, problematic situations have little chance of being resolved.

Three Examples of a Complaint Letter to follow:
- An unmarked version for study
- A marked version to study the placement of Toulmin elements and focus on the argument in the document
- A formatted version that shows the correct spacing between content areas in the letter

---

December 28, 2011

Mr. Larry Watkins, Sales Manager
Accurate Image Tees Incorporated
2311 Wilshire Ave.
Des Moines, IA 34778

Dear Mr. Watkins:

On January 7, 2012, I ordered a t-shirt from your company. Your online purchase policy states that goods that are defective or unsatisfactory can be returned with a money back guarantee.

When I received the t-shirt, the image on the face of it was distorted. The colors in the design were bleeding into each other which created more of a blur than an image of a humpback whale. On January 20, I returned the t-shirt to your company via the US Postal Service. I asked for a full refund of the purchase price.

One week later, I receive a letter from your company stating there would be no refund on the t-shirt. The letter went on to state that the company was not responsible for failure to follow washing instructions. It insinuated I washed the t-shirt and did not follow the care instructions; thereby, damaging the product.

I would like to protest this decision. I did not wash the t-shirt. Further, it is not possible to damage a silk-screen image in such a manner as to have the colors bleed into each other during the washing process. The worst that could be done would be shrinkage or fading.

I have purchased many theme t-shirts from your company and would like to remain a customer. I am sure that the Accurate Image Tees' return policy for defective goods was meant to include items that are defective. I would like to discuss this matter with you at your convenience in order to work out a fair adjustment. My telephone number is 254-773-2330; please call me with a time that I can meet with you.

Sincerely,

John Fowler

John Fowler

Figure: 5.16 Read-Only Version Complaint Letter

Legend

1. Dateline 1 inch below the top margin default which is 2 inches below the top of page.
2. 5 – 12 line spaces between the date and the inside address depending upon the length and style of the letter.
3. 1 line space between the inside address and the salutation.
4. 1 line space between the salutation and the first body paragraph.
5. 1 line space between each single spaced body paragraph.
6. 1 line space between the closing and the last paragraph.
7. 4 line spaces between the closing and the printed signature.

December 28, 2011 —①

②

Mr. Larry Watkins, Sales Manager
Accurate Image Tees Incorporated
2311 Wilshire Ave.
Des Moines, IA 34778

③

Dear Mr. Watkins:

④

On January 7, 2012, I ordered a t-shirt from your company. Your online purchase policy states that goods that are defective or unsatisfactory can be returned with a money back guarantee.

⑤ When I received the t-shirt, the image on the face of it was distorted. The colors in the design were bleeding into each other which created more of a blur than an image of a humpback whale. On January 20, I returned the t-shirt to your company via the US Postal Service. I asked for a full refund of the purchase price.

One week later, I receive a letter from your company stating there would be no refund on the t-shirt. The letter went on to state that the company was not responsible for failure to follow washing instructions. It insinuated I washed the t-shirt and did not follow the care instructions; thereby, damaging the product.

I would like to protest this decision. I did not wash the t-shirt. Further, it is not possible to damage a silk screen image in such a manner as to have the colors bleed into each other during the washing process. The worst that could be done would be shrinkage or fading.

I have purchased many theme t-shirts from your company and would like to remain a customer. I am sure that the Accurate Image Tees' return policy for defective goods was meant to include items that are defective. I would like to discuss this matter with you at your convenience in order to work out a fair adjustment. My telephone number is 254-773-2330; please call me with a time that I can meet with you.

⑥

Sincerely,

⑦— *John Fowler*

John Fowler

Figure: 5.17 Spacing Version

Legend

1. *Claim*
2. **Support** – Facts supporting the return of the defective product.
3. **Rebuttal** – Customer is rebutting the seller's response with a counter argument.
4. **Warrants** – Customer is addressing what she believes the seller assumes. This assumption would be loss of continued business if the matter is not resolved.

December 28, 2011

Mr. Larry Watkins, Sales Manager
Accurate Image Tees Incorporated
2311 Wilshire Ave.
Des Moines, IA 34778

Dear Mr. Watkins:

On January 7, 2012, I ordered a t-shirt from your company. Your online purchase policy states that goods that are defective or unsatisfactory can be returned with a money back guarantee.

(1) *When I received the t-shirt, the image on the face of it was distorted.* The colors in the design were bleeding into each other which created more of a blur than an image of a humpback whale. On January 20, I returned the t-shirt to your company via the
(2) US Postal Service. I asked for a full refund of the purchase price.

One week later, I receive a letter from your company stating there would be no refund on the t-shirt. The letter went on to state that the company was not responsible for failure to follow washing instructions. It insinuated I washed the t-shirt and
(3) did not follow the care instructions; thereby, damaging the product.

I would like to protest this decision. I did not wash the t-shirt. Further, it is not possible to damage a silk-screen image in such a manner as to have the colors bleed into each other during the washing process. The worst that could be done would be shrinkage or fading.

I have purchased many theme t-shirts from your company and would like to remain a customer. I am sure that the Accurate Image Tees' return policy for defective goods was meant to include items that are defective. I would like to
(4) discuss this matter with you at your convenience in order to work out a fair adjustment. My telephone number is 254-773-2330; please call me with a time that I can meet with you.

Sincerely,

John Fowler

John Fowler

Figure: 5.18 Toulmin Version

THE GOOD NEWS ADJUSTMENT LETTER

When Do You Write a Good News Adjustment Letter?

The Occasion arises when you are writing in response to a claim from a customer.

What's the PMB?

The Purpose The purpose of this letter is to tell the customer how you plan to handle the situation. You will also want to retain any future business. Therefore, strive to be fair and not quibble, be reasonable.

The Message Always begin with a congenial statement and accept regret. Even good news adjustment letters must be convincing. You may not think of it as an argument of sorts, but it is. You are arguing the integrity of your company. You are making the case to retain business with your company. In short, you must convince the customer that they are satisfied with the way you handled the claim, and that they must remain a customer.

Again, Toulmin will be needed. Your claim will be the acknowledgement of the failure and your desire to make restitution. Your support must be a statement that outlines the failure and how you will make things right. You will need to create a rebuttal. Most customers will assume their business is not that huge in the scheme of things. You must address this. Lastly, warrants must be placed as well. Warrants will address the unstated belief in the mind of the customer that you may not care to make a fair adjustment. You can also use warrants to make it clear your company values its customers. Carefully study the Toulmin sample to follow.

The Benefit What is the benefit of writing a letter of this type? You keep customers. You uphold the integrity of your business. You send a message that your customers are valued. Repeat business.

Three Examples of a Good News Adjustment Letter to follow:
- An unmarked version for study
- A marked version to study the placement of Toulmin elements and focus on the argument in the document
- A formatted version that shows the correct spacing between content areas in the letter

December 12, 2012

Mr. Ronald Smith
3432 Riley Lane
Dallas, TX 75243

Dear Mr. Smith:

Thank you for your letter of September 21, 2012. We apologize for the inconvenience you have experienced with the APX100 wireless printer. We deeply regret your loss of time and resources during this unfortunate event, and will make full restitution.

The software failure has been properly documented in our online trouble shooting web site. Additionally, our engineering department is in the process of redesigning the driver so that it will be compatible with earlier operating systems.

I am aware that our customer service department has already been in contact with you to arrange a complete refund of the purchase price. One of our product warranty associates will contact you in the near future with instructions on how to return the defective printer.

Please allow us to continue to be your main source when it comes to quality printers. In the spirit of this request, we are prepared to offer you a 20 percent discount on your next purchase. Know that we value our customers and pledge to continue providing the highest level of service you deserve. Not only do we strive for ultimate customer satisfaction, we work for it.

Sincerely,

Jack Anson

Jack Anson, Director of Sales
ABW Technologies

cc: Martin Burrows, Customer Service

Figure: 5.19 Read-Only Version Good News Letter

Legend

1. When there is no company letterhead, the date line must be 1 inch below the top margin default. This will put it at approximately 2 inches from the actual top of the page.
2. 5 – 12 line spaces between the date and the inside address depending upon the length and style of the letter.
3. 1 line space between the inside address and the salutation.
4. 1 line space between the salutation and the first paragraph.
5. 1 line space between single spaced body paragraphs.
6. 1 line space between the last paragraph and the closing.
7. 4 line spaces between the closing and the printed signature.
8. 1 line space between the printed signature/company title and the courtesy copy line

December 12, 2012 — ①

②

Mr. Ronald Smith
3432 Riley Lane
Dallas, TX 75243

③

Dear Mr. Smith:

④

Thank you for your letter of September 21, 2012. We apologize for the inconvenience you have experienced with the APX100 wireless printer. We deeply regret your loss of time and resources during this unfortunate event, and will make full restitution.

⑤

The software failure has been properly documented in our online trouble shooting web site. Additionally, our engineering department is in the process of redesigning the driver so that it will be compatible with earlier operating systems.

I am aware that our customer service department has already been in contact with you to arrange a complete refund of the purchase price. One of our product warranty associates will contact you in the near future with instructions on how to return the defective printer.

Please allow us to continue to be your main source when it comes to quality printers. In the spirit of this request, we are prepared to offer you a 20 percent discount on your next purchase. Know that we value our customers and pledge to continue providing the highest level of service you deserve. Not only do we strive for ultimate customer satisfaction, we work for it.

⑥

Sincerely,

⑦ — *Jack Anson*

Jack Anson, Director of Sales
ABW Technologies

⑧

cc: Martin Burrows, Customer Service

Figure: 5.20 Spacing Version

Legend

1. **Warrants** – An opening statement of congeniality that addresses the customers warrants. Those warrants would be his unstated belief that he has been inconvenienced.
2. **Claim** – This is an explicit statement that acknowledges the product failure. This is the claim
3. **Support** – These two paragraphs support the claim that there has been a product failure as well as an action plan to correct.
4. **Rebuttal** – This paragraph will rebut the customer's belief that the seller is not concerned with maintaining the customer's business. It goes further by offering future price breaks.
5. This last paragraph is additional warrants. The seller is still addressing unstated beliefs in the mind of the customer. This belief would be that the customer is of no value. The seller wishes to re affirm that the customer's business is of great value and promises future high levels of service.

December 12, 2012

Mr. Ronald Smith
3432 Riley Lane
Dallas, TX 75243

Dear Mr. Smith:

(1) — Thank you for your letter of September 21, 2012. We apologize for the inconvenience you have experienced with the APX100 wireless printer. *We deeply regret your loss of time and resources during this unfortunate*
(2) — *event, and will make full restitution.*

(3) — The software failure has been properly documented in our online trouble shooting web site. Additionally, our engineering department is in the process of redesigning the driver so that it will be compatible with earlier operating systems.

I am aware that our customer service department has already been in contact with you to arrange a complete refund of the purchase price. One of our product warranty associates will contact you in the near future with instructions on how to return the defective printer.

(4) — Please allow us to continue to be your main source when it comes to quality printers. In the spirit of this request, we are prepared to offer you a 20 percent discount on your next purchase

(5) — Know that we value our customers and pledge to continue providing the highest level of service you deserve. Not only do we strive for ultimate customer satisfaction, we work for it.

Sincerely,

Jack Anson

Jack Anson, Director of Sales
ABW Technologies

cc: Martin Burrows, Customer Service

Figure: 5.21 Toulmin Version

THE INQUIRY LETTER

When Do You Write an Inquiry Letter?

The Occasion   You write an inquiry letter to gather information. It could be information for research. It could be information to obtain employment. It could be information used in the 'bidding' process when awarding business to vendors. This last example is usually the most popular.

What's the PMB?

The Purpose   The purpose of this letter is to tell the customer how you plan to handle the situation. You will also want to retain any future business. Therefore, strive to be fair and not quibble, be reasonable.

The Message   You must quickly explain who you are and why you need the information.

It is important that you make your reasons clear for inquiry. Let's use a 'vendor inquiry' to fit the following example. Open with the traditional statement of congeniality, state your name and explain why you have chosen this particular vendor. You are already addressing warrants. You'll want to be complimentary as the vendor's unstated warrants will more than likely be 'they are the best in the field' if you are writing for information.

Clearly, Toulmin is in the middle of this. You may think an inquiry is a question. And what has a question to do with an argument. Here's the rub. Your reader must be convinced to provide the information you need. Remember, people in the business world have their own jobs and tasks. Answering an inquiry letter is something outside their normal duties and responsibilities. So you must make it worth their time. Here is where the Toulmin model kicks in. You have already stated warrants, now to the claim. In this case it will be a proposition which is the same thing. Proposition is a synonym of claim. In this case, your proposition or claim is your request. Be sure to write the request/proposition in such a way so that the reader will quickly understand he will get something in return. This is the key. THE READER OR VENDOR MUST THINK THEY WILL GET SOMETHING IN RETURN. HE MUST FEEL THAT ANSWERING THIS INQUIRY WILL BENEFIT HIM IN SOME WAY.

After you have stated your request, be specific about what information you need. Your support for the claim or proposition will be what the reader will benefit if he responds. Study the following model. It will help quite a bit. You will want to conclude with warrants or additional backing. Refer to the opening paragraph and elaborate. In the case of the example, putting business up for bid is an easy 'warrant' builder. Always remind the vendor that this will be a win-win situation. They may be awarded a huge contract. And if they perform, business will likely grow. Carefully study the Toulmin sample to follow.

The Benefit   What is the benefit of writing a letter of this type? You get valuable information either for locating a job, selecting a vendor, or research for new product development.

Three Examples of an Inquiry Letter to follow:
- An unmarked version for study
- A marked version to study the placement of Toulmin elements and focus on the argument in the document
- A formatted version that shows the correct spacing between content areas in the letter

March 3, 2012

Mr. Stanley Mackey
Global Account Manager
Overnight Freight Forwarders, Inc.
Maryville, TN 31209

Dear Mr. Smith:

I am writing to you because Overnight Freight Forwarders is one of the leaders in international shipping which comes as no news to you. I am sure you wish to grow your business as we wish to grow ours here at Davis Climate Systems.

My company has just signed a contract with an Italian automaker to ship five hundred auto air condition compressors per month to various factory locations in Europe. I am in the process of selecting an international freight forwarder and I am interested in hiring your company. Davis Climate Systems will be very good for Overnight Forwarders, but first we would need some basic information.

Would you be able to put together a proposal that would include volume discounted shipping rates, forwarding fees, and expedited transit times? All shipments will originate in Dallas, TX and be shipped to Frankfurt, Germany, Amsterdam, Netherlands, and Rome, Italy. Why will Davis Climate be good for your company?

Given the nature of our product, frequency of shipments, and destinations, a shipping contract of this caliber will be very lucrative. I dare say we will be one of your 'A' accounts. You would be our only freight forwarder. And as our European business expands, your business with us will expand. The number of air condition compressors that will be shipped will increase as we grow our business with the automaker. There are plans to increase shipments by 10% every quarter.

Clearly, this is a win-win situation for both our companies. I look forward to hearing from you. Because I will need to make a decision by March 31, I would greatly appreciate receiving your proposal before this date. Should you need additional information, you can reach me at my office, 800-356-8754.

Sincerely,

Jack Rossi

Jack Rossi, Logistics Manager
Davis Climate Systems, Inc.

Figure: 5.22 Read-Only Version Inquiry Letter

NOTES

Legend

1. Date line at top margin default
2. 5 – 12 line spaces between the date and the inside address depending upon the length of the letter.
3. 1 line space between the inside address and the salutation.
4. 1 line space between the salutation and the first paragraph.
5. 1 line space between each single spaced body paragraph.
6. 1 line space between the last paragraph and the closing.
7. 4 line spaces between the closing and the printed signature.

March 3, 2012 —(1)

(2)

Mr. Stanley Mackey
Global Account Manager
Overnight Freight Forwarders, Inc.
Maryville, TN 31209

(3)

Dear Mr. Smith:

(4)

I am writing to you because Overnight Freight Forwarders is one of the leaders in international shipping which comes as no news to you. I am sure you wish to grow your business as we wish to grow ours here at Davis Climate Systems.

(5)

My company has just signed a contract with an Italian automaker to ship five hundred auto air condition compressors per month to various factory locations in Europe. I am in the process of selecting an international freight forwarder and I am interested in hiring your company. Davis Climate Systems will be very good for Overnight Forwarders, but first we would need some basic information.

Would you be able to put together a proposal that would include volume discounted shipping rates, forwarding fees, and expedited transit times? All shipments will originate in Dallas, TX and be shipped to Frankfurt, Germany, Amsterdam, Netherlands, and Rome, Italy. Why will Davis Climate be good for your company?

Given the nature of our product, frequency of shipments, and destinations, a shipping contract of this caliber will be very lucrative. I dare say we will be one of your 'A' accounts. You would be our only freight forwarder. And as our European business expands, your business with us will expand. The number of air condition compressors that will be shipped will increase as we grow our business with the automaker. There are plans to increase shipments by 10% every quarter.

Clearly, this is a win-win situation for both our companies. I look forward to hearing from you. Because I will need to make a decision by March 31, I would greatly appreciate receiving your proposal before this date. Should you need additional information, you can reach me at my office, 800-356-8754.

(6)

Sincerely,

(7)— *Jack Rossi*

Jack Rossi, Logistics Manager
Davis Climate Systems, Inc.

Figure: 5.23 Spacing Version

Legend

1. **Warrants** – A congenial opening and a warrant that works on the assumption that the freight forwarder wants to grow more business and is looking for an opportunity.
2. *Claim* – This is the proposition you are putting forth. You want to convince the freight forwarder to submit a proposal for new business.
3. **The Requested Information** – this must always be included in an 'inquiry' letter.
4. **Support** – This information supports the claim or proposition that Davis Climate will be a good account for the freight forwarder
5. **Backing** – This statement backs up the unstated warrants in the first paragraph. The assumption being both companies wish to grow their business.
6. Specific deadline for the information.

March 3, 2012

Mr. Stanley Mackey
Global Account Manager
Overnight Freight Forwarders, Inc.
Maryville, TN 31209

Dear Mr. Smith:

(1) I am writing to you because Overnight Freight Forwarders is one of the leaders in international shipping which comes as no news to you. I am sure you wish to grow your business as we wish to grow ours here at Davis Climate Systems.

(2) My company has just signed a contract with an Italian automaker to ship five hundred auto air condition compressors per month to various factory locations in Europe. I am in the process of selecting an international freight forwarder and I am interested in hiring your company. ***Davis Climate Systems will be very good for Overnight Forwarders, but first we would need some basic information.***

(3) Would you be able to put together a proposal that would include volume discounted shipping rates, forwarding fees, and expedited transit times? All shipments will originate in Dallas, TX and be shipped to Frankfurt, Germany, Amsterdam, Netherlands, and Rome, Italy. Why will Davis Climate be good for your company?

(4) Given the nature of our product, frequency of shipments, and destinations, a shipping contract of this caliber will be very lucrative. I dare say we will be one of your 'A' accounts. You would be our only freight forwarder. And as our European business expands, your business with us will expand. The number of air condition compressors that will be shipped will increase as we grow our business with the automaker. There are plans to increase shipments by 10% every quarter.

(5) Clearly, this is a win-win situation for both our companies. I look forward to hearing from you. Because I will need to make a decision by March 31, I would greatly appreciate receiving your proposal before this date. Should you need additional information, **(6)** you can reach me at my office, 800-356-8754.

Sincerely,

Jack Rossi

Jack Rossi, Logistics Manager
Davis Climate Systems, Inc.

Figure: 5.24 Toulmin Version

THE REPRIMAND LETTER [PERFORMANCE AND TARDINESS]

When Do You Write a Reprimand Letter?

The Occasion You write a reprimand letter when an employee is not performing their job according to expectations. You are squarely in the middle of a disciplinary process.

What's the PMB?

The Purpose The purpose of this letter is to let the employee know that they are in a disciplinary process: certain changes in performance must be met, a timeline for improvement must be met, and documentation must be submitted. There are two example that follow this page, one reprimand for performance and one reprimand for tardiness.

The Message Understand that your message must be approved by Human Resources. They should be involved in this entire process. And again, this is clearly a situation where Toulmin must be included. You are making a case for poor performance or poor attendance. Your claim will be the statement citing poor performance or attendance. Your support will be all of the incidents that lead to this point. Rebuttals are important in this argument, remember, you are convincing the Human Resources Manager and the employee. At times, employees do not believe or cannot see that they are not meeting expectations.

This is why your support is very important. Be frank, but do not be bossy or condescending. This is an uncomfortable exercise for all. Be concise and maintain a tone that is empathetic. Yes, detail the 'faults,' but find time in the letter to address warrants. In this case, the unstated warrants in the employee's mind will be "what did I do?" "I want to be a good employee, but they cannot see it."

It is your turn to state these warrants and remind the employee that they are of value, you will help them improve and provide exact ways to make it happen. You will also have the opportunity to include rebuttals. Usually, employees will have excuses for poor performance or tardiness. You must address these and defuse them. Be sure to study the two example letters in this area. Rebuttals are extremely important. This letter must be your argument or 'case.' Do not loose control of it. If the employee counters your support to much, you will loose control and loose your case with Human Resources because it will not be clear to them that there is a problem.

The Benefit What is the benefit of writing a letter of this type? You may save a person's job. You are following Human Resources policies and procedures. You are protecting your own livelihood by having a strong employee team. And lastly, you are protecting yourself from civil litigation or what is commonly known as 'wrongful termination' or unfair employment practices.

Three Examples of Two Reprimand Letters to follow: Performance and Tardiness

- An unmarked version for study
- A marked version to study the placement of Toulmin elements and focus on the argument in the document
- A formatted version that shows the correct spacing between content areas in the letter

January 21, 2012

Mr. James Allen
Collins Electronic Company
Quality Assurance Department

Dear Mr. Allen:

Subject: Individual Evaluation – Performance Reprimand

We wish to thank you for your time at Collins Electronics this year. You are aware that our policy has been to ensure the best training of our employees in the belief that your success leads to the company's success.

Unfortunately, we regret to inform you that your job performance has not been satisfactory. This letter addresses performance ratings in two formal evaluations conducted over the past twelve months. During this time, your immediate supervisor rated your performance as 'does not meet expectations.' In each of these sessions, you were advised of specific areas in which to concentrate: software testing and software reclamation.

We will be putting you on retraining for three months. This will serve as your probationary period as per the policy of the company. Your immediate supervisor and a training associate will monitor your progress. Your improvement as reported by the training associate will satisfy the conditions for you to be removed from probationary status. If no improvement has occurred during this period, management has the right to terminate your employment.

If you have any concerns with regard to the probationary retraining period, please feel free to visit my office. I am confident you will put forth your best effort to improve your performance.

Sincerely,

George Bennett

George Bennett, Manager
Human Resources

cc: Tom Rawlins, Quality Assurance Manager
    Joshua Wheeler, Training Manger

Figure: 5.25 Read-Only Version for Performance Reprimand Letter

NOTES

Legend

1. Date – Begins at the 1 inch default for top margin.
2. 5 – 12 line spaces between the date line and the inside address depending upon the length and style of the letter.
3. 1 line space between the inside address and the salutation.
4. 1 line space between the salutation and the subject line.
5. 1 line space between each single-spaced paragraph.
6. 1 line space between the last paragraph and the closing.
7. 4 line spaces between the closing and the printed signature line. The area between the closing and printed signature create the 'signature block'
8. 1 line space between the signature clock and the CC Line

January 21, 2012 ——(1)

(2)

Mr. James Allen
Collins Electronic Company
Quality Assurance Department

(3)

Dear Mr. Allen:

(4)

Subject: Individual Evaluation – Performance Reprimand

We wish to thank you for your time at Collins Electronics this year. You are aware that our policy has been to ensure the best training of our employees in the belief that your success leads to the company's success.

Unfortunately, we regret to inform you that your job performance has not been satisfactory. This letter addresses performance ratings in two formal evaluations conducted over the past twelve months. During this time, your immediate supervisor rated your performance as 'does not meet expectations.' In each of these sessions, you were advised of specific areas in which to concentrate: software testing and software reclamation.

We will be putting you on retraining for three months. This will serve as your probationary period as per the policy of the company. Your immediate supervisor and a training associate will monitor your progress. Your improvement as reported by the training associate will satisfy the conditions for you to be removed from probationary status. If no improvement has occurred during this period, management has the right to terminate your employment.

If you have any concerns with regard to the probationary retraining period, please feel free to visit my office. I am confident you will put forth your best effort to
(5) improve your performance.

(6) Sincerely,

(7) *George Bennett*

George Bennett, Manager
Human Resources

(8)

cc: Tom Rawlins, Quality Assurance Manager
    Joshua Wheeler, Training Manger

Figure: 5.26 Spacing Version

Legend

1. **Congenial Opening.** This is your Warrants area. You are addressing the belief that the individual wishes to be thought of as a valued employee.
2. **Claim** – States the reason for the letter, a declaration that must be supported.
3. **Support** – Facts that support the claim. Highlights areas that must be improved.
4. **Rebuttal** – Defuses any counter-claim that the employee may raise with regard to fair employment practices.
5. **Ends on a positive note.** Re-dresses the belief that the individual wishes to be of value and continue to be employed. This is an additional Warrants area

January 21, 2012

Mr. James Allen
Collins Electronic Company
Quality Assurance Department

Dear Mr. Allen:

Subject: Individual Evaluation – Performance Reprimand

(1) We wish to thank you for your time at Collins Electronics this year. You are aware that our policy has been to ensure the best training of our employees in the belief that your success leads to the company's success.

(2) *Unfortunately, we regret to inform you that your job performance has not been satisfactory. This letter addresses performance ratings in two formal evaluations conducted over the past twelve months.* During this time, your immediate supervisor rated your performance as 'does not meet expectations.' In each of these sessions, **(3)** you were advised of specific areas in which to concentrate: software testing and software reclamation. .

(4) We will be putting you on retraining for three months. This will serve as your probationary period as per the policy of the company. Your immediate supervisor and a training associate will monitor your progress. Your improvement as reported by the training associate will satisfy the conditions for you to be removed from probationary status. If no improvement has occurred during this period, management has the right to terminate your employment.

(5) If you have any concerns with regard to the probationary retraining period, please feel free to visit my office. I am confident you will put forth the best effort to improve your performance.

Sincerely,

George Bennett

George Bennett,Manager
Human Resources

cc: Tom Rawlins, Quality Assurance Manager
      Joshua Wheeler, Training Manger

Figure: 5.27 Toulmin Version

January 21, 2012

Mr. James Allen
Collins Electronic Company
Commercial Sales

Dear Mr. Allen:

Subject: Individual Evaluation – Reprimand for Tardiness

I am sure you know that Collins Electronics has high standards for its employees. We believe you wish to be a successful employee. The company supports you in this endeavor. To that end, your overall performance is meeting expectations with the exception of one area.

Being prompt is essential for high level job performance. Supervisors routinely try to make allowances for unexpected issues that cause tardiness. However, your consistent tardiness has gone far past making allowances and is therefore not acceptable.

I have noticed your timesheets reflect an average of being 20 minutes late 4 days last week. This tardiness has been consistent over the last two months various days of the week. Because our customers are important to us, we would to like to implement the following course of action. You must come to the office 30 minutes early before doors open.

I am aware that you commute to work from Frisco which is not a short drive. Make sure you allow enough time to cover the miles factoring in traffic so that you can get to the office early. If there is an unexpected circumstance that will cause you to be late, please contact me immediately. Any further attendance issues in the future will result in disciplinary action.

I feel confident you will immediately improve your punctuality because I believe you want to make a valuable contribution to our company.

Sincerely,

Steve Mason

Steve Mason, Manager
Commercial Sales Department

Figure: 5.28 Read-Only Version Tardiness Reprimand Letter

NOTES

Legend

1. Date – Begins at the 1 inch default for top margin.
2. 5 – 12 line spaces between the date line and the inside address depending upon the length and style of the letter
3. 1 line space between the inside address and the salutation. 1 line space between the salutation and the subject line.
4. 1 line space between the subject line and the first paragraph.
5. 1 line space between each of the single spaced paragraphs.
6. 1 line space between the closing and the last paragraph.
7. 4 line spaces between the closing and the printed signature.

January 21, 2012 ──①

②

Mr. James Allen
Collins Electronic Company
Commercial Sales

③

Dear Mr. Allen:

④

Subject: Individual Evaluation – Reprimand for Tardiness

I am sure you know that Collins Electronics has high standards for its employees. We believe you wish to be a successful employee. The company supports you in this endeavor. To that end, your overall performance is meeting expectations with the exception of one area.

Being prompt is essential for high level job performance. Supervisors routinely try to make allowances for unexpected issues that cause tardiness. However, your consistent tardiness has gone far past making allowances and is therefore not acceptable.

I have noticed your timesheets reflect an average of being 20 minutes late 4 days last week. This tardiness has been consistent over the last two months various days of the week. Because our customers are important to us, we would to like to implement the following course of action. You must come to the office 30 minutes early before doors open.

I am aware that you commute to work from Frisco which is not a short drive. Make sure you allow enough time to cover the miles factoring in traffic so that you can get to the office early. If there is an unexpected circumstance that will cause you to be late, please contact me immediately. Any further attendance issues in the future will result in disciplinary action.

⑤

I feel confident you will immediately improve your punctuality because I believe you want to make a valuable contribution to our company.

⑥── Sincerely,

⑦── *Steve Mason*

Steve Mason, Manager
Commercial Sales Department

Figure: 5.29 Spacing Version

Legend

1. **Congenial Opening.** This is your Warrants area. You are addressing the belief that the individual wishes to be thought of as a valued employee because of his sales performance.
2. **Claim** – States the reason for the letter and serves as a declaration that must be supported later in the letter.
3. **Support** – facts that support the claim and provides an action plan for improvement.
4. **Rebuttal** – Diffuses and counter claim that the employee may use as a means to justify consistent tardiness and avoid taking responsibility.
5. **Backing** - Ends on a positive note. Re-dresses earlier warrants that the individual wishes to be of value. But most importantly, it addresses previous success which supports those warrants. This is BACKING. Backing supports Warrants.

January 21, 2012

Mr. James Allen
Collins Electronic Company
Commercial Sales

Dear Mr. Allen:

Subject: Individual Evaluation – Reprimand for Tardiness

(1) I am sure you know that Collins Electronics has high standards for its employees. We believe you wish to be a successful employee. The company supports you in this endeavor. To that end, your overall performance is meeting expectations with the exception of one area.

(2) Being prompt is essential for high level job performance. Supervisors routinely try to make allowances for unexpected issues that cause tardiness. ***However, your consistent tardiness has gone far past making allowances and is therefore not acceptable.***

(3) I have noticed your timesheets reflect an average of being 20 minutes late 4 days last week. This tardiness has been consistent over the last two months various days of the week. Because our customers are important to us, we would to like to implement the following course of action. You must come to the office 30 minutes early before doors open.

(4) I am aware that you commute to work from Frisco which is not a short drive. Make sure you allow enough time to cover the miles factoring in traffic so that you can get to the office early. If there is an unexpected circumstance that will cause you to be late, please contact me immediately. Any further attendance issues in the future will result in disciplinary action.

(5) I feel confident you will immediately improve your punctuality because I believe you want to make a valuable contribution to our company.

Sincerely,

Steve Mason

Steve Mason, Manager
Commercial Sales Department

Figure: 5.30 Toulmin Version

THE SALES LETTER

When Do You Write a Sales Letter?

The Occasion Sales letters are written when a product or service needs to be sold.

What's the PMB?

The Purpose The purpose of a sales letter is to convince or persuade. Sales letters secure business, retain business, and can announce new business.

The Message Sales letters can be highly specialized depending on the product or service being sold. And because the writer is convincing another party, Toulmin comes into play once again. Sales letters are arguments that persuade and convince. They will need to employ at least three to four Toulmin elements.

The claim is absolutely necessary because it states what you are trying to sell. It is the proposition being put forth. Support needs to be there because it offers facts that help the product or service to be enticing to the reader. Warrants must be included because sales letters should use a certain amount of audience psychology. Any buyer will have preconceived notions of what they want in a product. It is the writer's job to figure these out and address them in the letter. These as previously stated will be your warrants. These are the 3 most important Toulmin elements in the letter.

You may include a rebuttal. This would be optional because you must keep a sales letter brief. It cannot be too long. You will loose your reader. If you decide to use a rebuttal in a sales letter, you will need to refer to rival products or services and debunk their value. Use rebuttals sparingly. They have a tendency to be read as 'negative' posturing in a sales letter. It is best to focus on your good product or service rather than disparaging others.

The Benefit What is the benefit of writing a letter of this type? You are procuring new business. You are continuing a presence in the minds of loyal customers. You are announcing the acquisition of new products for sale. You are retaining current customers. In short, you are lengthening the life of your company.

Three Examples of a Sales Letter to follow:
- An unmarked version for study
- A marked version to study the placement of Toulmin elements and focus on the argument in the document
- A formatted version that shows the correct spacing between content areas in the letter

October 12, 2012

Ms. Janet Kolfax
Chairperson, English Department
Westbury College
Stamford, CT 80900

Dear Ms. Kolfax:

As chairperson of the English Department, no doubt you are very familiar with literature anthologies, and Caldridge Publishing. But are you ready to review an anthology that is the first collection focusing on African American 'passing narratives? *'Black crosses White is available and ready for shipment to your office. It is by far the best collection of narratives that deal with the anthropological issues surrounding bi-racial individuals in the late 18th and early 19th centuries.* And as you are already aware, the only collection.

Black crosses White was the first anthology to receive the Fulton Prize and has been adopted at four of the five top African American Studies Programs in the nation. All authors in the collection are couched in the African American Literature canon. The anthology also includes scholarly articles on each of the stories and a chapter on African American Literary Theory. Caldridge Publishing is also prepared to offer companion CDs with each anthology. This companion CD contains live readings of selected stories in the anthology.

We understand how difficult it is to adopt quality titles in a market where ethnic/racial literary works are few and far between. We also realize that you must be inundated with many offers from publishers promoting titles. *But how many are truly unique and original in approach? Black crosses White decrease your selection process substantially.* Please take the time to fill out and return the request card for your desk examination copy today. If you have any questions, please feel free to call me at any time, 800-237-1111.

Thank you,

Paul Green

Paul Green, Area Manager
Caldridge Publishing Co.

Figure: 5.31 Read-Only Version

Legend

1. Date on top margin default
2. 5 – 12 line spaces between the date line and the inside address depending upon the length and style of the letter.
3. 1 line space between the inside address and the salutation.
4. 1 line space between the salutation and the first body paragraph.
5. 1 line space between each single spaced body paragraph.
6. 1 line space between the last body paragraph and the closing.
7. 4 line spaces between the closing and the printed signature.

October 12, 2012 ——(1)

(2)

Ms. Janet Kolfax
Chairperson, English Department
Westbury College
Stamford, CT 80900

(3)

Dear Ms. Kolfax:

(4)

As chairperson of the English Department, no doubt you are very familiar with literature anthologies, and Caldridge Publishing. But are you ready to review an anthology that is the first collection focusing on African American 'passing narratives? 'Black crosses White is available and ready for shipment to your office. It is by far the best collection of narratives that deal with the anthropological issues surrounding bi-racial individuals in the late 18th and early 19th centuries. And as you are already aware, the only collection.

(5)

Black crosses White was the first anthology to receive the Fulton Prize and has been adopted at four of the five top African American Studies Programs in the nation. All authors in the collection are couched in the African American Literature canon. The anthology also includes scholarly articles on each of the stories and a chapter on African American Literary Theory. Caldridge Publishing is also prepared to offer companion CDs with each anthology. This companion CD contains live readings of selected stories in the anthology.

We understand how difficult it is to adopt quality titles in a market where ethnic/racial literary works are few and far between. We also realize that you must be inundated with many offers from publishers promoting titles. But how many are truly unique and original in approach? Black crosses White decrease your selection process substantially. Please take the time to fill out and return the request card for your desk examination copy today. If you have any questions, please feel free to call me at any time, 800-237-1111.

(6)—— Thank you,

(7)—— *Paul Green*

Paul Green, Area Manager
Caldridge Publishing Co.

Figure: 5.32 Spacing Version

Legend

1. *Claim or Proposition* – states clearly that the anthology is the best available.
2. **Support** – Facts that support the anthology being the best.
3. **Warrants** – These sentences address the assumption that the chairperson is very busy during adoption season and may not say so. This would be an address of unstated warrants. *Note that the writer uses phrasing insinuates his anthology will decrease the search.*

October 12, 2012

Ms. Janet Kolfax
Chairperson, English Department
Westbury College
Stamford, CT 80900

Dear Ms. Kolfax:

As chairperson of the English Department, no doubt you are very familiar with literature anthologies, and Caldridge Publishing. But are you ready to review an anthology that is the first collection focusing on African American 'passing narratives? *'Black crosses White is available and ready for shipment to your office. It is by far the best collection of narratives that deal with the anthropological issues surrounding bi-racial individuals in the late 18th and early 19th centuries. And as you are already aware, the only collection.*

Black crosses White was the first anthology to receive the Fulton Prize and has been adopted at four of the five top African American Studies Programs in the nation. All authors in the collection are couched in the African American Literature canon. The anthology also includes scholarly articles on each of the stories and a chapter on African American Literary Theory. Caldridge Publishing is also prepared to offer companion CDs with each anthology. This companion CD contains live readings of selected stories in the anthology.

We understand how difficult it is to adopt quality titles in a market where ethnic/racial literary works are few and far between. We also realize that you must be inundated with many offers from publishers promoting titles. *But how many are truly unique and original in approach? Black crosses White decrease your selection process substantially.* Please take the time to fill out and return the request card for your desk examination copy today. If you have any questions, please feel free to call me at any time, 800-237-1111.

Thank you,

Paul Green

Paul Green, Area Manager
Caldridge Publishing Co.

Figure: 5.33 Toulmin Version

EXERCISES:

Choose **[1]** of the following writing options. This is an exercise in writing an arguable claim letter. Review the examples of Toulmin and spacing requirements. You will need to include Toulmin elements of argumentation in this letter.

It should be composed in block format. Refer to the textbook or posted example.

Option 1

As a student in a state college, you learn that your governor and legislature have cut next year's operating budget for all state colleges by 20 percent. This cut will cause the firing of faculty members; drastically reduce admissions, financial aid, and new programs. Write an arguable claim letter to your governor or representative expressing your strong disapproval and justifying a major adjustment in the proposed budget.

Option 2

Write an arguable claim letter about a problem you've had with goods or service. State your case clearly and objectively, and request a specific adjustment.

Image © alexskopje, 2013. Used under license from Shutterstock, Inc.

HIRED!

HOW TO WRITE PERSUASIVE JOB APPLICATION LETTERS AND RESUMES

OVERVIEW

Take a moment to answer the following questions. Why are you interested in persuasive business writing? How will you use this skill? What do you hope to gain?

What you want is what almost everybody wants in the business world. You want your ideas to be accepted by your peers and bosses. You want to be appreciated. You want to be perceived as a smart effective go-getter that's not afraid to promote your best abilities. Why? Because as a go-getter, you'll get to the finish line to claim your prize. And remember, every persuasive document has *PMB:* a purpose, a persuasive message, and a positive benefit.

USING THE TOULMIN MODEL TO WRITE PERSUASIVE JOB APPLICATION LETTERS

Yes, back to the Toulmin Model. Writing persuasive job application letters is one of the most direct ways to use this model to your benefit. Don't forget that Toulmin sells. It sells ideas and recommendations, projects, proposals, and possibilities. In this case, TOULMIN SELLS YOU!

Toulmin in the Toolbox

We need tools to fix a variety of things, say perhaps, fixing up your future to be everything you want it to be, promising! In any given workplace, every employee should have a personal tool box, that is, a repository of skills that will help you to be successful such as good time management skills, organization skills, and analytical skills. Think of the Toulmin Model as another type of toolbox. If you remember, there are six elements in Toulmin. You do not have to include all six in a business document. Three are mandatory: claim, support, warrants. Three are optional: rebuttal, backing, qualifiers. In the case of job application letters, the three mandatory elements are essential. But above all, keep your application letter to ONE PAGE.

The Three Essentials:

CLAIM   SUPPORT   WARRANTS [audience]

The Beginning of the Letter – Consider this your opening paragraph.

Claim – Your claim is a straightforward declarative statement. It will contain three key pieces of information: the job for which you are applying, some knowledge of the company that has opened the position and a reference to 'you as the perfect fit.' Here's an example:

> *I am writing to apply for the project management position in systems research. Martin Electronics is widely known for its advancements in commercial robotics systems. I am convinced my experience, education, and enthusiasm will be of great benefit to your company.*

The Middle of the Letter—Consider this the body. It should be no longer than a second or third paragraph.

Support – There are two approaches you may take.

> *If you currently hold a job,* this part should emphasize your work experience. The support for your claim will be your prior job experience that addresses the specific requirements of the position. It can also include certifications, special skills like speaking more than one language, computer software, or any other special training that will speak to your credibility as a viable candidate for the job.

If you are recently graduated from college, emphasize your academic record, special coursework, assistantships, awards, community service, or extra curricular activities.

Whichever approach you use, always write to what you believe is the employer's main interests. At the same time, support your claim. That is, focus on the evidence that promotes you as the best person for the job.

The End of the Letter – Consider this your last paragraph.

<u>Warrants</u> – Remember, warrants mean audience. Your readers are your audience. Warrants are very important because they will address the expectations of your audience which may be a prospective employer. You should make it your priority to know what employers value most. Every perspective employer will have unstated expectations over and above the basic requirements. For example, an employer will expect you to report to work on time and not abuse breaks and lunch hours. This is a given and is not usually found on a list of job requirements. When you write your warrants, you will need to figure out what those unstated expectations will be and explain how you will fulfill them. So if we're dealing with timeliness to work and at work, you would write a sentence something like this:

My excellent time management skills not only help in meeting project deadlines, they ensure reporting to work on time and keeping to scheduled lunch hours and breaks.

Closing Lines

Make sure you request an interview. Include times of availability and be sure to reference possible interview times 'at your employer's convenience.'

If my credentials are to your satisfaction, I would welcome an interview at any time that is convenient for you. My schedule is very flexible. Please phone or email any afternoon.

Example: A typical application letter highlighting Toulmin Elements

Read and study the illustration on the following page. Note the 3 key pieces of information in the claim, concise discussion of experience and education for support, and the closing warrants paragraph.

Legend

1. Claim
2. Support
3. Warrants
4. Closing Lines

345 Ridge View Dr.
Cambridge, MA 66435
May 5, 2013

Mr. Joe Logan
Director of Human Resources
Martin Electronics, Incorporated
Boston, MA   66754

Dear Mr. Wells:

(1) I am writing to apply for the project management position in prototype design. Martin Electronics is widely known for its advancements in commercial robotics systems. I am convinced my experience, education, and enthusiasm will be of great benefit to your company.

(2) In addition to holding a Master's Degree in Electronic Engineering, I have five years experience as an electronics engineer. I have spent these years working in systems design, practical and theoretical applications testing, and advanced robotics research. I understand how to move a project from inception to adoption. It requires expertise in the field, effective team building techniques, and excellent time and resource management.

(3) My goal is to help advance your business, to be productive, effective, and get results. Being able to motivate colleagues to complete projects on time is only one of my assets. I consider myself a creative inventor, an excellent communicator, an adept problem solver, and a specialist in process analysis. Most importantly, I understand Martin Electronics wants employees committed to the company's success.

(4) If my credentials are to your satisfaction, I would welcome an interview at any time that is convenient for you. My schedule is very flexible. Please phone or email any afternoon.

Sincerely,

Robert Groom

Enclosure: Resume

Figure 6.1 Application Letter with Toulmin Elements

STRATEGIES FOR WRITING SUCCESSFUL JOB APPLICATION LETTERS

Good Practices: They Should Be Persuasive, Adaptive, Succinct, and Confident

Write a letter that persuades
Persuade – Create a sample job application letter that can be modified to fit a specific job. Your major selling points should be embedded in the 3 Toulmin elements: claim, support, and warrants.

Write a letter than can be adapted
Adapt – Modify the letter to fit a specific job. Make sure you tie your education/experience [support] to the job requirements. Make sure you tie your qualifications or personal qualities [warrants] to the employer's expectations.

Write a letter that is succinct
Succinct – Be clear and concise. Keep your letter to one single-spaced page.

Write a letter that speaks confidence
Confident – Be confident in your tone. Present an enthusiastic image of yourself by making sure the letter represents you in the best possible light.

BAD PRACTICES: Avoid the following behaviors

- **Avoid Exaggeration**
  Do not overly exaggerate your abilities with flamboyant language. Keep your 'superego' out of it. It's okay to convey confidence, simply temper it with a little common sense. Don't go overboard.

- **Avoid Bragging**
  Do not brag about past achievements. Listing them is fine. Avoid telling a narrative that positions you as the 'super hero' that can save the world.

- **Avoid Gold-Digging**
  Do not discuss salary options. Talking about or suggesting salary is a non-starter. This discussion is only broached when an actual offer is being made.

- **Avoid the 'I' Crazies**
  Do not over use 'I.' Don't go crazy with the letter 'I.' It's okay to write your letter in first person, but avoid prefacing everything from this perspective. It can be redundant and sound egotistical.

- **Avoid Copying**
  Do not use templates. There are many out there. Be aware that human resource professionals can spot them easily. Be original by using your own voice. It will demonstrate interest and initiative.

4 TYPES OF PERSUASIVE APPLICATION LETTERS:

- Response to Advertisement
- General Inquiry Letter
- Targeted Inquiry Letter
- Follow Up Letters
  - Post Interview Letter
  - No Response Letter

Response to Advertisement Letter

Remember that your letter must include the minimum mandatory Toulmin elements: claim, support and warrants. The opening paragraph should contain your **claim** which will serve as an introduction. You should identify yourself as an applicant for the opening. You should state the specific position. You should also include some information that implies you have knowledge of the company. To gain extra attention, you can refer to a manager or executive in the company only if you have permission to do so.

The body of your letter should be spent in **support** of your claim. This area should not exceed 2 paragraphs. This is the backbone of your argument. Remember, this letter is persuasive and should argue the case of 'YOU' being hired to fill the position. If you are currently a student, stress your academic record, student activities, and personal and community interests. If you are currently employed, stress job experience, education and training, and special skills.

The conclusion of your letter should be spent on '**warrants**'. This area is crucial. This is where you stress your qualities that most employers want to see in their employees. These are not normally listed in the 'job requirements'. They can be things like communication skills, an enthusiastic personality, and team building abilities. Warrants can be success items that employers would most likely want to see some contribution from you such as your desire to grow the business, motivate other employees, or increase productivity. Keep these letters to one page only.

Study the Toulmin and Spacing Examples Figure 6.2 and 6.3 – For a closer understanding of how to write and format this type of letter.

General Inquiry and Targeted Inquiry Letters

A general inquiry letter will also need to include a claim, support, and warrants area. It differs from the response to a job posting in the opening paragraph. There will not be a specific position available upon which to build your **claim**. So you will need to refer to a department such as '*future positions available in the accounting group.*' Or in the case of a targeted inquiry, refer to the '*future possibility of hiring an accounting professional.*'

Example General Inquiry Claim

> *Please review my qualifications for a position in your account-*
> *ing department. My Bachelor's Degree in Accounting, Masters in*
> *Business Administration, and graduate internship with Boyd &*
> *Young has prepared me to be a productive member of your firm.*

Example Targeted Inquiry Claim

> *Does your company need a seasoned manager in accounts receiv-*
> *able with eight years experience, proven commitment, and*
> *customer service experience? If so, please consider the enclosed*
> *application materials.*

Review the job-specific letter explanation for guidelines on the body [support] and the conclusion [warrants]. These areas in a general inquiry and targeted inquiry letter should be written in basically the same manner as a job-specific letter. Keep this letter to one page only.

Study the Toulmin and Spacing Examples Figures 6.4 thru 6.7 – For a closer understanding of how to write and format these types of letter.

Follow Up Letters

At first glance, you might think your job has been done once you fire off your cover letter and resume, in other words, the selling is all in the cover letter and the resume. Not true. You can continue to sell yourself in a follow up letter.

Follow up letters are essential. The best use for these types of letters is to thank your employer for an interview, the second to obtain acknowledgement of having received your materials should you not hear anything from the hiring manager.

These letters can continue to make the case that you are the best hire for the job. Each of them will have the three mandatory Toulmin elements: claim, support, and warrants.

- **Post-Interview Letter**

Write a follow up letter post interview if you have not heard anything within one week. The post-interview letter is much like a second interview because you have another opportunity to get your name in front of the hiring manager, another opportunity to make your case by briefly touching on your qualifications. How is this Toulmin? You are restating *your claim* that you are the best, and providing brief evidence of it, *the support*. It also gives you another opportunity to address any unstated beliefs or values your interviewer may have held about you or what was expected in a new employee, *the warrants*.

- **No-Response Letter**

The purpose of this letter is to force a confirmation of receipt. It is important that you know the prospective employer has received your cover letter and resume. Write a no-response letter if you have not received a confirmation of receipt from the prospective employer within 10 days. A no-response letter is still a persuasive document. It restates your case for employment by presenting your resume and cover letter a second time, and it reiterates your claim for hire, the reasons that support you as the most capable, and warrants which will address the expectations of the employer. Keep the letter brief and to the point.

Study the Toulmin Examples Figures 6.8 thru 6.9 – For a closer understanding of how to write and format these types of letters.

Legend

1. Start the return address at the 1 inch default for the top margin.
2. 4 line spaces between the return address and the inside address.
3. 1 line space between the inside address and the salutation.
4. 1 line space between the salutation and the first paragraph. The body paragraphs should be single-spaced.
5. 1 line space between all of the body paragraphs.
6. 1 line space between the final paragraph and the closing.
7. 4 line spaces between the closing and the printed signature.
8. 1 line space between the printed signature and the enclosure-resume line.

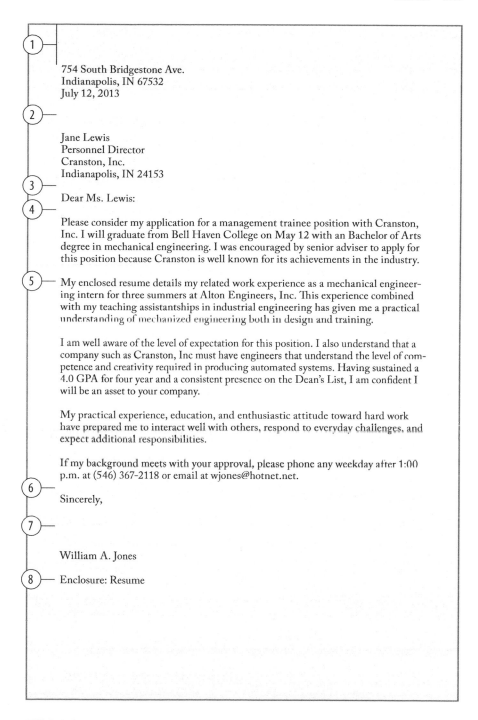

754 South Bridgestone Ave.
Indianapolis, IN 67532
July 12, 2013

Jane Lewis
Personnel Director
Cranston, Inc.
Indianapolis, IN 24153

Dear Ms. Lewis:

Please consider my application for a management trainee position with Cranston, Inc. I will graduate from Bell Haven College on May 12 with an Bachelor of Arts degree in mechanical engineering. I was encouraged by senior adviser to apply for this position because Cranston is well known for its achievements in the industry.

My enclosed resume details my related work experience as a mechanical engineering intern for three summers at Alton Engineers, Inc. This experience combined with my teaching assistantships in industrial engineering has given me a practical understanding of mechanized engineering both in design and training.

I am well aware of the level of expectation for this position. I also understand that a company such as Cranston, Inc must have engineers that understand the level of competence and creativity required in producing automated systems. Having sustained a 4.0 GPA for four year and a consistent presence on the Dean's List, I am confident I will be an asset to your company.

My practical experience, education, and enthusiastic attitude toward hard work have prepared me to interact well with others, respond to everyday challenges, and expect additional responsibilities.

If my background meets with your approval, please phone any weekday after 1:00 p.m. at (546) 367-2118 or email at wjones@hotnet.net.

Sincerely,

William A. Jones

Enclosure: Resume

Figure: 6.2 Response to an Advertisement Block-Style – formatting guidelines

Legend

1. Writer identifies self and purpose. **THIS IS THE CLAIM.**
2. Writer relates specific qualifications from his resume to the job opening. **THIS IS THE SUPPORT.**
3. Writer addresses the expectation level of the employer demonstrating knowledge of what the writer feels the employer wants in an employee. **THESE ARE YOUR WARRANTS. This paragraph can also contain relevant interests.**
4. Writer continues to address areas he feels the employer wants in a strong applicant. **THIS IS BACKING** for the warrants. This area should focus on soft skills.
5. Follow up statement. Keep it short and simple.

754 South Bridgestone Ave.
Indianapolis, IN 67532
July 12, 2013

Jane Lewis
Personnel Director
Cranston, Inc.
Indianapolis, IN 24153

Dear Ms. Lewis:

(1) Please consider my application for a management trainee position with Cranston, Inc. I will graduate from Bell Haven College on May 12 with an Bachelor of Arts degree in mechanical engineering. I was encouraged by senior adviser to apply for this position because Cranston is well known for its achievements in the industry.

(2) My enclosed resume details my related work experience as a mechanical engineering intern for three summers at Alton Engineers, Inc. This experience combined with my teaching assistantships in industrial engineering has given me a practical understanding of mechanized engineering both in design and training.

(3) I am well aware of the level of expectation for this position. I also understand that a company such as Cranston, Inc must have engineers that understand the level of competence and creativity required in producing automated systems. Having sustained a 4.0 GPA for four year and a consistent presence on the Dean's List, I am confident I will be an asset to your company.

(4) My practical experience, education, and enthusiastic attitude toward hard work have prepared me to interact well with others, respond to everyday challenges, and expect additional responsibilities.

(5) If my background meets with your approval, please phone any weekday after 1:00 p.m. at (546) 367-2118 or email at wjones@hotnet.net

Sincerely,

William A. Jones

Enclosure: Resume

Figure: 6.3 Response to an Advertisement Block Style - Toulmin Version

Legend

1. Return address begins at 1 inch top margin default. It is centered in the document given the left and right margins. Each line should be left-justified.
2. 6 line spaces between the return address and the inside address.
3. 1 line space between the inside address and the salutation.
4. 1 line space between the salutation and the subject line. Subject line must be underscored.
5. 1 line space between the subject line and the first paragraph.
6. 1 line space between each single spaced paragraph.
7. 1 line space between the last paragraph and the closing.
8. 4 line spaces between the closing and the printed signature.
9. 1 line space between the printed signature and the enclosure notation
10. The return address and the signature block should be centered horizontally and aligned on the left.

① ② ③ ④ ⑤ ⑥ ⑦ ⑧ ⑨ ⑩

642 Eagle Lane
Eugene, OR 97405 ⑩
June 20, 2012

Marlon Walters, Personnel Director
Ernst & Anderson, Inc.
555 Mellow Street
Seattle, WA 82290

Dear Mr. Walters:

INQUIRY: Management Position in the Real Estate with Your Company

Please review my qualifications detailed in my cover letter and resume. If there are any prospective job openings with your firm in the future, I would appreciate an opportunity. My Bachelor's Degree in Accounting, Masters in Business Administration, and three years with Boyd & Young has prepared me to be a productive member of your firm.

My background in macro economics, cost/benefit analysis, and real estate law have given me an excellent foundation in real estate finance. This combined with my professional experience in internal auditing, accounts receivable/ payable, accounting systems analysis and financial reporting have given me the skills and practical experience you would seek.

As a volunteer member of the Small Business Foundation, I have taken part in fund raising and on site training for future small business owners. Working with the local Chamber of Commerce, I helped organize events to promote the exceptional business environment in Seattle. If you would like an -in-person visit to explore my qualifications, I would welcome an interview.

My references will establish me as a confident team player that does not shy away from additional responsibilities.

Sincerely,

Carol R. Chasone

Encl: Resume

Figure: 6.4 General Inquiry Letter Modified Block Style - Spacing Version.

Legend

1. Focusing on his experience and relying on his skills previously stated, the writer plainly asks for a job. ***THIS IS THE CLAIM.*** *The claim is simply...Hire me because I have the experience and skills you seek.*
2. Relates information from resume to employer's needs. ***THIS IS SUPPORT.***
3. The writer wants to highlight the skills he believes the employer would desire in an applicant. ***THIS IS A WARRANT*** because the writer is making assumptions about the employers beliefs. He then makes the connection between the skills he thinks the employer deems valuable and himself.
4. Encourages follow up

642 Eagle Lane
Eugene, OR 97405
June 20, 2012

Marlon Walters, Personnel Director
Ernst & Anderson, Inc.
555 Mellow Street
Seattle, WA 82290

Dear Mr. Walters:

INQUIRY: Management Position in Real Estate Group with Your Company

(1) Please review my qualifications for a management position in your real estate group. My Bachelor's Degree in Accounting, Masters in Business Administration, and three years with Boyd & Young has prepared me to be a productive member of your firm.

(2) My background in macro economics, cost/benefit analysis, and real estate law have given me an excellent foundation in real estate finance. This combined with my professional experience in internal auditing, accounts receivable/ payable, accounting systems analysis and financial reporting have given me the skills and practical experience you would seek.

(3) As a volunteer member of the Small Business Foundation, I have taken part in fund raising and on site training for future small business owners. Working with the local Chamber of Commerce, I helped organize events to promote the exceptional business environment in Seattle. My references will establish me as a confident team player that does not shy away from additional responsibilities.

(4) If an opening exists or if you would like an in-person visit to explore my qualifications, I would welcome an interview.

Sincerely,

Carol R. Chasone

Encl: Resume

Figure: 6.5 General Inquiry Letter Block Style - This example shows Toulmin elements.

Legend

1. Return address begins at 1 inch top margin default. It is centered in the document given the left and right margins. Each line should be left-justified.
2. 6 line spaces between the return address and the inside address.
3. 1 line space between the inside address and the salutation.
4. 1 line space between the salutation and the subject line. Subject line must be underscored.
5. 1 line space between the subject line and the first paragraph.
6. 1 line space between each single spaced paragraph.
7. 1 line space between the last paragraph and the closing.
8. 4 line spaces between the closing and the printed signature.
9. 1 line space between the printed signature and the enclosure notation.
10. The return address and the signature block should be centered horizontally and aligned on the left.

(1)

642 Eagle Lane
Eugene, OR 97405 —(10)
June 20, 2012

(2)

Marlon Walters, Personnel Director
Ernst & Anderson, Inc.
555 Mellow Street
Seattle, WA 82290

(3)

Dear Mr. Walters:

(4)

INQUIRY: Management Position in Real Estate Finance with Your Company

(5)

Does your company need a seasoned manager in your real estate finance with
eight years experience? My Bachelor's Degree in Accounting, Masters in Business
Administration, and three years with Boyd & Young has prepared me to be a
productive member of your firm.

My background in macro economics, cost/benefit analysis, and real estate law have
given me an excellent foundation in real estate finance. This combined with my
professional experience in internal auditing, accounts receivable/ payable, accounting systems analysis and financial reporting have given me the skills and practical
experience you would seek.

As a volunteer member of the Small Business Foundation, I have taken part in
fund raising and on site training for future small business owners. Working with
the local Chamber of Commerce, I helped organize events to promote the excep-
(6) — tional business environment in Seattle.

My references will establish me as a confident team player that does not shy away
from additional responsibilities. If an opening exists or if you would like an in-
person visit to explore my qualifications, I would welcome an interview.

(7)

Sincerely,

(8)

Carol R. Chasone

(9)

Encl: Resume

Figure: 6.6 Targeted Inquiry Letter Modified Block - Use this letter when making an
inquiry for a specific position. This example also shows the formatting requirements.

Legend

1. Focusing on his experience and relying on his skills previously stated, the writer plainly asks for a job. *THIS IS THE CLAIM. THE CLAIM IS SIMPLY....Hire me because I have the experience and skills you seek.*
2. Relates information from resume to employer's needs. *THIS IS SUPPORT.*
3. The writer wants to highlight the skills he believes the employer would desire in an applicant. *THIS IS A WARRANT* because the writer is making assumptions about the employers beliefs. He then makes the connection between these skills he thinks the employer deems valuable and himself.
4. Encourages follow up.

642 Eagle Lane
Eugene, OR 97405
June 20, 2012

Marlon Walters, Personnel Director
Ernst & Anderson, Inc.
555 Mellow Street
Seattle, WA 82290

Dear Mr. Walters:

INQUIRY: Management Position in Real Estate Finance with Your Company

(1) Does your company need a seasoned manager in your real estate finance with eight years experience? My Bachelor's Degree in Accounting, Masters in Business Administration, and three years with Boyd & Young has prepared me to be a productive member of your firm.

(2) My background in macro economics, cost/benefit analysis, and real estate law have given me an excellent foundation in real estate finance. This combined with my professional experience in internal auditing, accounts receivable/ payable, accounting systems analysis and financial reporting have given me the skills and practical experience you would seek.

(3) As a volunteer member of the Small Business Foundation, I have taken part in fund raising and on site training for future small business owners. Working with the local Chamber of Commerce, I helped organize events to promote the exceptional business environment in Seattle. My references will establish me as a confident team player that does not shy away from additional responsibilities.

(4) If an opening exists or if you would like an in-person visit to explore my qualifications, I would welcome an interview.

Sincerely,

Carol R. Chasone

Encl: Resume

Figure: 6.7 Targeted Inquiry Letter Block Style -Use this letter when making an inquiry for a specific position. This example shows Toulmin elements.

Legend

1. Always reference the position and the date employment materials were forwarded.
2. *Warrant* – This sentence serves two purposes. It conveys friendliness and it is also a warrant. You are identifying with what may be a difficult time for the hiring manager. Identification is a powerful tool when trying to reach an intended audience.
3. *Claim* – You are stating you are the best candidate and should be hired.
4. *Support* – Evidence to support your claim of being the best candidate. Holding advanced degree with experience.
5. Closing thank you and request for information.

345 Ridge View Dr.
Cambridge, MA 66435
May 5, 2013

Mr. Joe Logan
Director of Human Resources
Martin Electronics, Incorporated
Boston, MA 66754

Dear Mr. Wells:

(1)— I applied for the project manager position at Martin Electronics on July 2. I have no confirmation that you received my materials. Perhaps they (2)— were lost in the postal system or misplaced in your offices. The hiring process can be very hectic. I am enclosing additional copies of my letter and resume.

(3)— If a decision has not been made, *I remain convinced that my qualifications make me the "best fit."* Finding candidates that hold an advance degree in (4)— engineering is rare. This combined with direct on the job experience is also exceptional.

(5)— Thank you for the opportunity and I look forward to hearing from you soon.

Sincerely,

Robert Groom

Enclosure: Resume

Figure: 6.8 No Response Application Letter Block Style – This letter is considered a follow up letter when no confirmation is received after having forwarded application materials. The Toulmin Elements: claim, support, and warrants are present.

Legend

1. Opening Statement of congeniality. Always convey thanks.
2. *Warrants* – You are identifying with the employer. You are addressing unstated concerns that hiring managers may have. When you address privately held beliefs, you are identifying. This is a very powerful warrant.
3. <u>Claim</u> – You are restating the claim that you should get the job.
4. *Support* – References background and resume details when qualifications are mentioned
5. *Warrant* – You are addressing an unstated belief that all hiring managers want employees that are willing to deal with any special conditions like excessive overtime.
6. Closing thank you and request for information.

345 Ridge View Dr.
Cambridge, MA 66435
May 5, 2013

Mr. Joe Logan
Director of Human Resources
Martin Electronics, Incorporated
Boston, MA 66754

Dear Mr. Wells:

(1) — Thank you for allowing me the opportunity to speak with you last
Wednesday. *I am well aware of the competitive nature of the job market.*
(2) — *Locating a good pool of candidates, vetting and interviewing them must be a
slow methodical process.*

(3) — Because of this, <u>I remain confident in the knowledge that my education,
experience, and post-graduate training will be of great benefit to your</u>
(4) — <u>company.</u> Because Martin Electronics has an excellent reputation for
hiring highly capable individuals, *I am certain my qualifications are best*
(5) — *suited for the project manager position.* For this opportunity, you would be
hiring an employee willing to put in the hours regardless how many, to get
the job done.

(6) — Again, thank you for your interest. I look forward to hearing from you in
the near future.

Sincerely,

Robert Groom

Enclosure: Resume

Figure: 6.9 No Response Application Letter Block Style - This letter is considered a
follow up letter when no confirmation is received after having forwarded application
materials. The Toulmin Elements: claim, support, and warrants are present.

RESUMES
And the Toulmin Model of Persuasion

Resumes are an instant snapshot of an applicant. We like to hope employers take the time to slowly study a resume. Some studies say only one to two minutes are spent reading through the resume. Other scenarios paint a picture of a prospective employer thoughtfully going through each detail and carefully weighing the evidence against the job requirements.

Realistically, there is no sure answer. What is sure, however, is the weight your resume will carry. Persuasive job application letters do some of the heavy lifting by getting the employers attention, giving them some insight into you and what you may bring to the table. This is chiefly due to the tone with which you write the letter, the way in which you use 'warrants' to address unstated expectations, and the information you choose get the employer's interest quickly.

The resume closes the deal so to speak. It is a document of support. It supports the initial image you created for yourself in the letter. The letter and the resume work in tandem. Both are persuasive and both use the Toulmin to do the persuading.

Therefore, you must be careful to accurately reflect the 'letter' picture you have painted of yourself in the resume. Again, your resume is the 'hard evidence' that will persuade the employer you are the person for job. It will answer the proverbial question they all ask themselves, "*Is this person the right person for the job?*"

The three essential Toulmin elements are also present in resumes. Resumes have specific parts or information that can be organized in different ways. What you present and how you present it can act as a **'claim,'** as **'support'** and as **'warrants.'**

THE PARTS OF A RESUME AS TOULMIN ELEMENTS

Contact Information

Always include your name, address, phone number, and email. Avoid informal email handles such as 'superdude. Create a professional image.

Career Objective Area of Expertise

The Claim You can choose either one of the following: career objective or area of expertise. Consider both your 'claim' to the job. You are letting your employer know what job you want and why you will be perfect for it.

Education, Skills, Certifications, Work Experience

The Support Your level of education, skills that are relevant to the job, certifications that prove competence on the job, and most importantly, **your actual work experience.** All of this information supports your claim that you are the perfect person for the job and should be hired.

Competencies, Achievements, Personal Data and Interests, References

The Warrants Your competencies, achievements on the job, personal interests, community service, hobbies, and references will address the unstated questions an employer may have and cannot ask. Present information that will give them a good idea of the type of employee you will turn out to be. Warrants can be embedded in the following.

Contact Information can be Warrants: Though this is not considered part of the Toulmin model. It is very valuable. It gives your prospective employer a way to contact you. This is basic and is always located at the top of your resume. It must include your name, address, phone number, and email address. Keep the email address professional. Use your name and not 'whacky' handles such as *nascarguy@bcc.net* that will project a poor image.

Career Objective or Area of Expertise can be a Warrant: This information tells your employer the specific job you wish to have and it can also help him to see where you may be able to fit into the company. An objective should specify the job you seek in a general way if you are entry level or a targeted way if you have been in the workforce for a period of time. Your objective can be written to persuade as in the **Targeted Persuasive Objective** or it can simply let the employer know the job in which you are interested.

Here's a **General Objective** for entry level positions:

Objective: A position in General Accounting

Here's a **Targeted Objective** for management positions:

Objective: A management position in General Accounting

Here's a **Targeted Persuasive Objective** that will specify the job you want at the same time making a strong claim that you are the best possible 'fit' having eight years experience.

Objective: To apply eight years of logistics management in international and domestic shipping with your company

Here's a **Targeted Long-Term Objective** that will specify the job and imply long term goals. It helps your employer to know you are planning a long term future with the company.

Objective: Seeking a position in Systems Analysis that leads to management.

Here's an **Area of Expertise** line: This is also an objective though it does not literally say that it is. Always use the phrase "Area of Expertise" instead of 'Objective. The type of approach will focus on two or three main strengths. You will position this line where your objective would normally be. An area of expertise line is appropriately used in 'qualifications' resumes. Here's two:

Area of Expertise: Performance and Process Improvement/ Training/Management

Area of Expertise: Process Improvement/Import/Export Management

Education This is the section that lists your diplomas, degrees, or advanced degrees. List your most recent first. Always list the type of degree, area of study, the school, and the date you graduated.

<u>Bachelor of Science, International Studies, 2005</u>
    Walton College, Newark, NJ
<u>Master of Business Administration, 2007</u>
    Bridgetown University, Baltimore, Maryland

Work Experience Your work experience should list all of the relevant jobs that will help you land the one you are after. If you have ten past jobs and only four of them are relevant to the job you are seeking, use the four relevant one. Each listing of your job should include the name of the company, your position, the date you were employed at the company, and your specific job responsibilities.

Skills This can be used as section to itself. Use it to highlight special skills like speaking foreign languages and competence in office software systems.

Certifications Use this section if you additional certifications in your field such as: Advanced Systems analysis, Certified Notary, Certified Mediator, or having completed a course in Professional Salesmanship.

Competencies These are additional skills that demonstrate your ability to manage a team of people and get results. Things such as time management, project management, effective negotiating, excellent communication.

Achievements Achievements/awards/accomplishments demonstrate you as an innovator that follows through and is successful in improving process and solving problems. It could be things such as:

- Compiled procedures manual for transportation department
- Designed and implemented import procedures for client base and import personnel
- Designed and implemented procedures for cargo tracing: import and export

Personal Data and Interests List any community involvement that may have afforded you some awards. List any personal activities or interests that are relevant to the position you are seeking. List memberships in professional organizations. You can also list hobbies that may be of interest to the employer.

References Do not list your references on your resume, but compose a list of them on a separate document. At the end of your resume, conclude with this line:

References Available upon Request

Should the employer wish to see them, you will already have them prepared to forward. Before you use someone as a reference, be sure to get there permission. Reference letters are also very strong tools to promote your good character. If you decide to collect reference letters, keep them in a portfolio that can be easily transmitted to the employer. Also, make sure they are timely. Try not to have five or ten year old letters. Make sure they are relatively recent.

WRITING THE 'RIGHT' RESUME

Rule 1 – Be Flexible, but DO NOT INVENT OR DISTORT YOUR QUALIFICATIONS

One resume does not fit all. Be prepared to make subtle changes in your content.

Just as you were advised to tailor your application letters to the job, you must also do so with your resume. It is rare that a job opening will match your qualifications in every way. You must figure out ways to write your qualifications so that they match the job as closely as possible.

- **First Thing** – Create a prototype resume. Do not attempt to write a finished version. You need a basic model that lists your education, work experience, and workplace skills. Print a hard copy.

- **Second Thing** – Locate the job description and requirements. Print a hard copy. Research the company online, print whatever you find.
- **Third Thing** – Place your prototype resume, the job description/requirements, and the researched information about the company on your desk in front of you. Read over everything. Have a clear idea of what will be expected of you, and what you can offer.
- **Fourth Thing** – Take time to decide which resume style will be the best vehicle: chronological, functional, or qualifications.
- **Fifth Thing** – Afterward, think of ways to profile yourself for the job. That is, figure out the type of employee that is implied in the job description. In your mind, you will need to 'become' this person. You will need to align yourself as much as possible to the job requirements. This will require a great amount of creativity because you should not distort or invent information.
- Locate as many common threads between you and the job as possible. The endgame is to convince the prospective employer you are well-suited for the position.
- **Last Thing** – Draft your resume to showing how your background and qualifications will benefit the company.

STYLE

There are three commonly used resume formats. The difference between them is what information you choose to emphasize and how you choose to organize it. They are:

- The Reverse Chronological Resume
- The Functional Resume
- The Qualifications/Achievements Resume

Study the examples of these resumes, Figures 6.10 - 6.12

The Reverse Chronological Resume places emphasis on work experience and education. It presents your education from the most recent degree to the oldest, and your work experience from the most recent job to the oldest. In short, begin with the most recent in either case or work backward in time.

The Functional Resume places emphasis on skills. It will focus on three to four areas that will be particularly relevant or important for the job you seek. This type of resume 'cuts to the chase'. It keeps the employer from sifting through lines of work experience to figure out if experience translates into real skills needed on the job. This resume will group skills together that are directly related to the job. It is easy to read and easy for the employer to figure out if you are a good fit in a short amount of time.

This type is also good for people who have held many relevant jobs but due to the length, they cannot be listed chronologically. The functional resume can present the basic skills from those many jobs in a concise manner.

The Qualifications/Achievements Resume places emphasis on competence. Its organization creates an image of you as a capable and knowledgeable worker. It presents hard information and facts that support the qualifications profile you create. It can also showcase outstanding character traits that will increase your value as a prospective employee.

Substance: What Information Should be Present

- Know what the job requires and what will be expected of You
- Know your strengths
- Know your weaknesses

Based on this information, bring your work history, background, and education into the mix. You will have a good idea of the area you want to emphasize to help you land the job.

Wanna emphasize experience and education? ➡ **The Reverse Chronological Resume**

Wanna emphasize skills? ➡ **The Functional Resume**

Wanna emphasize competence? ➡ **The Qualifications/ Achievements Resume**

Form And Function: Tips for Writing Effective Resumes

- **No One Stop Shopping** – Do not depend on one version of your resume. It is rare to find job openings that fit individual qualifications in every way. Tailor the content of your resume to the job.
- **No Bling** – Do not create extravagant imagery. Keep to one color, black. Avoid accent colors or highlights. Do not try to be artsy with symbols or shapes. Do not use colored paper, keep your document white or pale grey. Bottom line, keep it simple and tasteful.
- **No Encyclopedias** – Try to keep your resume to one page. If your resume appears very cramped and you cannot edit out information, go to a second page.
- **No Flashy Font Styles** – Stay conservative. Use New Times Roman, Arial or Calibri. These are widely used and easy to read.
- **No Variations in Font Size** – Your font size for the body should range between 10 and 12 point. Pick one size and stick to it for consistency. Your font size for headings should not be greater than 14 point.

- **No Extreme Designs** – Do not be excessive in your use of lines, boxes, underlining, bullets, symbols and italics
- **No Whacky Email Handles** – Use your name, RSmith appropriate.com, not spaceman@outtasink.com
- **No Informal language** – Do not use slang expressions Do not use contractions.
- **No use of "I"** – Do not write in first person, write in 3rd person consistently throughout the document.
- **No Grammatical or Spelling Errors** – Do not depend on Spell/Grammar Check. The software does not catch word usage errors, missing words, or grammar errors consistently. Always proofread your document at least two times. Read it aloud at least two times. Reading aloud will help you detect grammar errors.

GUIDELINES for Formatting Resumes

HEADING
- Heading should contain name and contact information.
- Heading should be positioned at the top margin default, approximately 1 inch below the top edge of the page, and single-spaced.
- There should be a border below the heading to separate it from the body of the resume.

CONTENT
- All content sub-headings should be aligned on the left margin default, approximately 1 inch from the left edge of the page, and should be in bold.
- Content areas in the body of the resume should be single-spaced.
- There should be only one line space between all content areas.

MARGINS
- Margins should be at the 1 inch default.

FONT
- Use one font style only and keep typeface size to 12', not smaller than 11'.

BULLETS
- Depending on the style and length of the resume, you can manually align your content directly underneath the sub-heading, then use the tab defaults to move the text over. Or you can simply highlight the content and use the 'bullet' point function on the tool bar.

Jack S.Turner

1538 Carroll Ave. Boston, MA 76392   Phone: (453)-874-8882   Email: jturner@fast.net

Objective	To apply three years of logistics experience to a management position in international business and trade.

Management Skills

- Warehouse and Inventory management
- Managed selection of domestic and international carriers
- Managed selection of customs brokers and freight forwarders
- Managed import shipment routing
- Responsible for internal training of transportation personnel

Process Improvement Skills

- Compiled procedures manual for transportation department
- Redesigned cargo claims procedures with corporate interface
- Developed and implemented import procedures transportation personnel
- Developed and implemented procedures for cargo tracing: import and export
- Developed and implemented export procedures for freight forwarders

Documentation Skills

- International purchase order processing
- Bill of Lading processing
- Processing and audit of freight invoices
- Generated domestic and international shipping documentation
- Statistical reporting on cost, container usage, carrier service.

Education	Bachelor of Science, International Studies, 2005 Walton College, Newark, NJ Master of Business Administration, 2007 Bridgetown University, Baltimore, Maryland
Certifications	International Shipping Documentation Import Documentation Effective Negotiating
Employment	Manager, Logistics, Baird Industries, Boston, MA, 2009 – present Manager, Import Operations, Alton Inc, Newark, NJ 2004 – 2009
References	Available on request

Figure: 6.10 Print Resume in Functional Skills Format   Emphasizes skills instead of employment history

Jack S. Turner
1538 Carroll Ave. • Boston, MA 76392
Phone: (453)-874-8882 • Email: jturner@fast.net

Objective	To apply three years of operations and documentation experience to a management position in international business and trade
Education	Master of Business Administration, 2007 Western Maryland University, Louisville, MD
	Bachelor of Science, International Studies, 2005 Walton College, Newark NJ
Competencies	Process Improvement • Problem Solving • Training Facilitation
Experience	Manager, Transportation Logistics, Baird Pharmaceuticals, Boston, MA 2009 – Present

- Warehouse and Distribution Management
- Evaluated and selected domestic and international carriers
- Generated domestic and international shipping documentation
- Compiled procedures manual for transportation department
- Responsible for internal training of transportation personnel

Manager, Import Operations, Alton Automotive Inc, Newark, NJ 2004 – 2009

- Designed and implemented import procedures for client base and Import personnel
- Generated customs documentation and managed customs clearances
- International purchase order processing
- Managed import shipment routing
- Processing and audit of freight invoices
- Statistical reporting on container usage, shipment cost and carrier service levels.

Workplace Skills	Microsoft Word • Outlook • Power Point • Excel • Access • Publisher • Photoshop

Certifications

- International Shipping Documentation
- Import Documentation
- Effective Negotiating

Interests	Fencing, Gourmet Cooking, Competitive Cycling, Yoga
References	Available on request

Figure: 6.11 Print Resume in Reverse Chronological format   Emphasizes a stable pattern of work experience beginning with the current job and working backward.

NOTES

Legend

1. Claim - Areas of Expertise
2. *Warrants - Qualifications*
3. Support - Education
4. *Warrants - Competencies*
5. Support - Experience
6. *Warrants - Achievements*
7. Support - Experience
8. *Warrants - Achievements*

Jack S. Turner

1538 Carroll Ave. Boston, MA 76392   Phone: (453)-874-8882   Email: jturner@fast.net

(1) — *Areas of Expertise: Process Improvement/Import-Export Management*

Qualifications Highlights

Multi-Lingual logistics professional with 6+ years in international shipping and doc-umentation. Developed and implemented departmental procedures for domestic and international shipping. Expert level knowledge of domestic and international ship-ping documentation. Sound experience in carrier selection and management. Highly experienced in pricing negotiations with carriers. Proficient in statistical reporting

(2) — of shipping expense, level of service, container usage, and marine insurance.

Education

Bachelor of Science, International Studies, 2005 Walton College, Newark, NJ
Master of Business Administration, 2007 Bridgetown University,

(3) —   Baltimore, Maryland

Competencies

(4) — *Time* & Project Management   Problem Solving   Excellent Communication

Professional Experience

Manager, Transportation Logistics, Baird Pharmaceuticals, Boston, MA,
2009 – present

- Evaluated and selected domestic and international carriers, customs bro-kers and freight forwarders
- Compiled procedures manual for transportation department
- Responsible for internal training of transportation personnel

(5) — *Achievements:*

(6) —
- *Compiled procedures* manual for transportation department

Manager, Import Operations, Alton Automotive Inc, Newark, NJ   2004 – 2009

- Generated customs documentation and managed customs clearances
- International purchase order processing
- Managed import shipment routing
- Processing and audit of freight invoices

(7) —
- Statistical reporting on shipment cost, container usage, and carrier service levels.

Achievements:

- *Designed and implemented import procedures for client base and import personnel*

(8) —
- *Designed* and implemented procedures for cargo tracing: import and export

Certifications

International Shipping Documentation   Import Documentation
   Effective Negotiating

Systems Software Skills

Microsoft Word, Outlook, Power Point, Excel, Access, Publisher, Photoshop

Figure: 6.12 Print Resume in Qualifications Format   Toulmin Version - Emphasizes key persuasive elements.

EXERCISES

These are exercises in identification, composition, and formatting. You will be required to assume the 'Jack Turner' identity below. Read the narrative, identify your key information and compose each letter in a persuasive manner.

1. Using information from the narrative below, compose one ***response to an advertisement*** application letter in block format as if you are 'Jack Turner'. Include three Toulmin elements: claim, support, and warrants.

2. Keeping your 'Jack Turner' identity, compose one ***post-interview*** follow-up letter in modified block format. Include three Toulmin elements: claim, support, and warrants.

My name is Jack S. Turner. Right now I live in Houston in an apartment on Jamison Ave., but not for long if I don't find a job before I finish school. My dream job would be to work as a logistics manager for a major international container shipping line. I can't expect to walk right into this job, so settling for an entry level management position may be within reach. I'll graduate college in December from Rice University with a B.A. in International Business. I know my experience is pretty close to what companies might want given I'm just finishing school and haven't had much direct experience. I did land an intern position APL Lines the summer of 2008 where I worked in export documentation and created international bills of lading for global accounts. I learned all about shipping lanes, how goods are rated for shipping cost, insurance, arrival times, and even restrictions on goods going to certain countries. During the summer of 2007, I worked at the same shipping line but as a dock worker loading shipping containers. It's a good thing there is a port in Houston, I would not have been able to learn about commercial merchant ships, the speed, the design, the crew compliment, and loading the containers. I even learned how the ships are loaded using cranes that run alongside the ships, how they are secured for storms at sea, and how they are manifested aboard the ship.

I'm hoping my summer jobs will be enough to land a good entry level position because it's rare to have related skills for your dream career right after you graduate. Both summer experiences really helped me to see that international shipping is more than just filling out paperwork. There's a lot to learn when it comes to the actual physical work that is involved, the ships that carry the goods, and the high risk of shipping over the ocean rather than by air. Just wearing a tie or nice trousers looks good, but it's also good to be able to say I loaded the container. I know about commercial ships and ocean travel. In other words, I've gotten my hands dirty learning from the bottom up. I bring relevant experience to the table so my dream employer won't have to worry about training me after I hopefully get hired. Besides, I'm disciplined, energetic, and a quick-learner. Yea, I feel pretty good about myself given the economy. So good, I'll write to the human resource offices in the states at two major container shipping lines line Maersk and Evergreen.

Image © OPOLJA, 2013. Used under license from Shutterstock, Inc.

STATUS PLEASE!

SHORT INFORMAL REPORTS IN THE WORKPLACE

Reports can be informational or analytical. In this section, we will focus on five informational reports: progress report for business, progress report for a term project, periodic activity report, feasibility report, and meeting minutes.

PERSUADE ME!

Yes, certain reports can be persuasive.

Four of the five in this section can be highly persuasive.

- progress report for business
- progress report for a term project
- the periodic activity report
- the feasibility report

Each of these reports will contain three Toulmin Elements: a claim, support, and warrants. They are embedded in the PMB: purpose, message, and benefit.

Within the purpose, you will find the claim, within the message you will find the support, within the benefit you will find warrants.

| Purpose = Claim | Message = Support | Benefit = Warrants |

PERSUASIVE PROGRESS REPORTS:
Business and Academic Term Projects, perhaps indent it under the main PERSUASIVE PROGRESS REPORTS

Business

Progress reports sometimes referred to as status reports are essential because they are making a case for the successful completion of a task. They must be highly persuasive because they are used to measure the progression toward a specific goal. They are also used to evaluate various projects within an organization. Remember, you are 'selling' your success on a particular project.

The way in which you report your progress has much to do with the impression you create in the mind of your supervisors. In effect, your progress report is arguing your ultimate success. In this sense, not only must you use Toulmin, that is, have a specific claim, you must support that claim with evidence that argues you will complete your task successfully and on time. These reports are usually informal and are created as-needed.

There are internal and external progress reports. Within a business organization or academic institution, internal progress reports are typically operational. They can be used to track delays, monitor the completion of an activity, or used to assess proposed timelines, or gauge the effectiveness of a particular initiative. But remember, the way in which you report your progress can be persuasive.

It's all in the 'writing' of the document. On the following pages, an example illustration will show how Toulmin elements can be used to make the report persuasive. Always format your documents according to the design layout in the illustrations.

The same can be said for external progress reports which are given to clients. They too, must be highly persuasive. They are used to show how monetary resources are being used. They can also provide information that can determine the viability of a specific project. Ultimately, clients want know two things. They wish to know if a project will be completed according to schedule and within the confines of the budget. It will be your job to convince them that success is just around the corner.

Academic Term Projects

Term project progress reports are also very similar in concept. Like the business progress report, they measure progression toward a specific goal. They are purely internal and used as a means of communication between student and professor. They have three big purposes. First, they must convince a professor to see the quality of a student's term project. Second, they must convince the professor that the student has a clear picture of what must be done and when it must be done. It also helps to convince the professor that the student has command of the material. As you probably already know, deadlines are as much a part of college as they are a part of business. Term project progress reports map out a 'work completed' progression, they note work that is in progress, work that is completed, and any possible complications that may threaten the scheduled due date.

There will also be an example illustration to show how Toulmin elements work within the report. Always format your document according to the design layout in the illustrations.

GUIDELINES for Progress Reports

- Always follow the design layout precisely.
- Always Use an Appropriate Tone. Do not be overly informal even though these reports are considered informal. It should be optimistic and not negative. Does not use slang expressions, contractions, or inflammatory language.
- Create a Clear and Concise Subject Line. As with email and memos, give your reader a reason to want to read your report by keeping it short, too the point, and interesting.
- Report Honestly. Even if you are not going to meet your projected deadlines, or stay within budget, do not panic. Calmly explain why you will not meet the date, or why you exceeded budget. Do not distort information.
- Organize Your Information for Readability. Try to keep the length to $1 - 1/12$ pages. Group your information together in a logical sequence with sub-headings. Use bullets or numbered lists so that your managers or professors can read through the information quickly.
- Timelines are crucial. Progress reports are steps toward an intended goal. In business or in school, these goals are always confined to timeframes. There must be a beginning and ending date; otherwise, why would it be call a progress report? Progress means progressing toward some end.

MEETING MINUTES

Minutes constitute an official record of a meeting. These meetings can occur on the job, at school, in the community center, even in your home. They are a tool for any organization be it a committee, work group, project team, or advisory council. In short, they are a chronicle of what happened.

Therefore, they must be accurate. They should be clear and comprehensive. They should be objective and sterile in tone. They should never record emotional exchanges that will spread negative light on the attendees. Meeting minutes should objectively record discussed business in a positive sterile manner.

They should never interpret. They should only report. At times, meetings will veer away from the established agenda. This can make the reporting difficult. If this occurs, never be reluctant to ask the person calling the meeting to slow down or clarify what the unintended detour means.

Meeting minutes are always distributed to the attendees and at times other higher ranking management. Take care to write your document as if the CEO of the company, the president of the university, or the head of whatever organization is on the distribution list.

Therefore, you should adhere to all of the rules of business writing. If you use a template in a word processing program, make sure the basic content areas are addressed. Templates are good in that you can use them on site at the meeting if you have a lap top. This will prevent you from having to transcribe the minutes at a later date.

Basic Content Area for Meeting Minutes

These side-headings should always be used and the document should be formatted according to the design layout in the illustrations.

Type of Meeting:

Meeting Called By:

Note Taker:

Members Present:

Agenda Topics:
- Call to Order
- Approval of the Minutes
- New Business
- Discussion Items
- Action Items

Adjournment:

GUIDELINES for Writing Meeting Minutes

General
- Always complete writing the minutes directly after the meeting. Do not rely on your memory. You will inevitably leave information out or misinterpret what you thought was discussed.
- Pay attention and take good notes if you do not have a laptop and template.
- Make the minutes Readable. Use headings and lists. Write them clearly and succinctly.
- Stay away from personal commentary. Remember, do not interpret the proceedings. Record objectively.
- Record all agenda items, action items, and any conclusions.
- Do not forget to list and distribute the document to all of those who attended the meeting.
- If you use a template, cross reference the content areas with those in the following example. Be thorough. Templates vary in style and content. When choosing a template, not only should you cross reference the content areas with those in the example, keep to a conservative professional design. NO bling.

Formatting
- Manage your tone. Do not write your personality into the document.
- Keep your document free of grammatical and spelling errors.
- Format your document appropriately with the proper content headings, margin settings, font size and style found in the example if you do not elect to use a template.
- Keep the size to 12 point, the style to a conservative, 'New Times Roman,' 'Ariel Narrow' or 'Calibri.'

PERSUASIVE PERIODIC ACTIVITY REPORTS

Periodic activity reports can be persuasive just as progress reports can be. You must remember that the workplace demands optimum efficiency from its employees. So yes, it's great if you are doing the best job you can do, most of your colleagues know it as you interact on a daily basis, and for the most part your immediate supervisor is aware of it too. Not enough.

Your hard work and efficiency needs to be documented, and not just in your yearly evaluations, but as often as possible. Reports give you the opportunity, and periodic activity reports will do just that. They are written, documented accounts of your good work. In them, you are reporting on your activities, your tasks, your ideas, all that pertains to eventual success. So think of them as mini-arguments for your future promotions. Yes, they must report your activities on a specific project, but they must also sell 'you' as the best of the best. Think of these reports as a means by which to persuade your supervisor or boss that they have hired the best person for the position, and the next person due for promotion. And again, it's Toulmin. Each time you lay out the particulars to a project you have been working on, you must sell the success of that project and that means using Toulmin effectively. Your claim will be a clear statement of how the project will lead to a positive future outcome. It will also reiterate the purpose of the project which is inherently beneficial to the company.

The details of your work as listed in a periodic activity report are the support, the evidence of your hard work. This support will reinforce your claim that the project is viable and beneficial to the company in the long run.

The benefits section in the report is the warrants, very important. As I've said before with regard to your reader or your boss or the audience… they are all the same…your mission is to appeal to what YOU THINK their unstated beliefs may be.

GUIDELINES for Periodic Activity Reports

- Always provide a clear subject line.
- Always provide an 'overview' section that will review the purpose of your activities for your reader.
- Always include specific activities within a specific timeframe. Always provide the names of principal individuals with whom you come in contact during these activities.
- Always put your best forward. When detailing specific activities, outline your key accomplishments and report any other relevant activity that has bearing on your project.
- Always conclude with a 'benefits' area that will answer the expected question, what will the company gain in terms of image and/or revenue from this venture?

PERSUASIVE FEASIBILITY REPORTS

All persuasive business documents begin with a claim and argue the claim by means of support, audience warrants, and occasionally some rebuttals. In the case of a feasibility report, not only will you be arguing a claim, you will be arguing the feasibility of the claim.

Feasibility reports help bosses, supervisors, and executives make decisions. It could be a decision on a course of action, an idea, a solution to a problem, or an improvement to a process. In the workplace, good employees will always have ideas that will fix what needs to be fixed, but not all of these ideas will be viable.

That is, not all of them will be the correct course of action needed to solve a problem. This is where feasibility reports come into play. They are succinct, persuasive documents that evaluate the feasibility of certain ideas.

For example, a company is having problems meeting its payroll. In order to make sure they will have adequate funds, a short term fix would be to eliminate the night shift. Yes, this would be immediately successful in the short term, but in the long term, it could impact customers because productivity levels would have dropped and it could impact employee morale.

A feasibility report would provide some answers to obvious questions in this scenario:

- How do we deal with the cash flow situation?
- What courses of action do we have to deal with this situation?
- Could there be some negative fallout, or will there by positive effects?
- What are the benefits of this course of action, what are the risks?
- Does this situation require immediate action, or can we deal with it later?

THE FEASIBILITY REPORT: 6 Sections with Guidelines
The section title must be used as a sub-heading.

Subject Line The subject line must be clear and succinct. Be sure to use the word 'feasibility.' It should state the exact issue on which the report focuses.

Background Include background information that summarizes the situation, states the problem, and/or poses questions of feasibility.

Recommendation The recommendation should explicitly provide a possible solution[s] to the problem quickly. It should also provide a 'rationale' for the solution[s].

Alternatives Because other options are considered in a feasibility report, this area should provide an alternative solution[s]. This will allow the reader to decide which course of action is the most feasible.

Suggested Action   The most feasible alternative is argued in this part. It should provide relevant details, data, and any other criteria available. This support should be arranged to persuade the reader to accept the recommended solution.

Overall Feasibility   This is the conclusion of the argument, the area in which a feasible solution is presented. It will weigh the alternatives in terms of positives and negatives. This section should be written to arrive at the most feasible solution and present benefits.

MEMO

To: Jerry Summers, President
           West Highland University
From: Janice Poland, Chair, African American Program
           Steering Committee

Subject: **Progress Report on the African American Studies Program**

Summary
On January 20, the president of the university authorized the creation of an African American Studies program. The projected completion date is May 15, 2013 with plans to have the program up and running fall of 2013. Thus far, we have completed Task 1 and Task 2 of the three proposed tasks.

Work Completed
February, 2013
Task 1 – Create steering committee, draft degree plan, recruit faculty
February represented a significant milestone in the creation of our new African American Studies program. A basic framework of the program was put together and will serve as a strong base from which to move forward.

- The steering committee was formed. Committee is composed of eight members that represent administration, admissions/registrar, faculty, and advisors.
- The emphasis degree has been designed by the steering committee in tandem with the Vice President of Instruction.
- Five faculty members have agreed to teach in the program to cover five disciplines: English, Sociology, History, Government, and Humanities.
- Agreement made with 'Student Life and Affairs' office to sponsor 2 entertainment programs each semester to focus on African American Culture.

February, 2013
Task 2 – Brand the program and select the college in which it will be housed
The following month produced a home for the new home and brand for the program. The logistics for supporting the program are in place, as well as a small marketing strategy to recruit students.

- Agreement was reached to house the African American Studies program in the College of Humanities.
- Professional Support Staff have been hired to schedule and input the courses in DataCall to be available in the online schedule of courses.
- The college communications and graphics department have branded the program. The following promotional materials have been created: pamphlets, posters, course flyers, and bulletin boards [2] to be placed in high traffic areas on campus.

Figure: 7.1 Typical Business Progress Report in the Workplace

continued on next page

Work Remaining

Task 3 – Obtain District Approvals and Articulation Agreements

We will need to concentrate on getting approvals of the emphasis degree and the certificate of study for those students who wish to have documentation on their transcripts while holding degrees in other disciplines such as Business Management. The scenario would be: Bachelor of Business Management with certification in African American Studies. The following need to happen.

- The District Curriculum Committee will need to approve the emphasis degree in African American studies.
- The certificate in African American Studies will need to be approved by the District Curriculum Committee.
- Research Articulation Agreements with other universities: Lawton University, The State University of Texas, and the West Texas State.

At this time, the establishment of the African American Studies program is on schedule. The steering committee understands that the program must be launched fall 2013. We have all indications that the degree and certification approvals will come to fruition. We have also begun conversations on articulation with department chairs on our targeted institutions.

Figure: 7.1 Typical Business Progress Report

NOTES

Legend

1. Single space all content sections
2. ½ inch between the To: From: Subject: side headings and the content lines. Align the content lines at the left.
3. 1 line space above and below the subject line.
4. Bold the subject line
5. Single space all paragraphs. Bold the sub-heading.
6. 1 line space between each content area.
7. Single space the paragraph and bold the sub-headings.
8. Use bullets to be concise.
9. Single space and bold the sub headings.
10. Use bullets to be concise.

MEMO

To: Jerry Summers, President
West Highland University
From: Janice Poland, Chair, African American Program
Steering Committee

Subject: **Progress Report on the African American Studies Program**

Summary
On January 20, the president of the university authorized the creation of an African American Studies program. The projected completion date is May 15, 2013 with plans to have the program up and running fall of 2013. Thus far, we have completed Task 1 and Task 2 of the three proposed tasks.

Work Completed
February, 2013
Task 1 – Create steering committee, draft degree plan, recruit faculty
February represented a significant milestone in the creation of our new African American Studies program. A basic framework of the program was put together and will serve as a strong base from which to move forward.

- The steering committee was formed. Committee is composed of eight members that represent administration, admissions/registrar, faculty, and advisors.
- The emphasis degree has been designed by the steering committee in tandem with the Vice President of Instruction.
- Five faculty members have agreed to teach in the program to cover five disciplines: English, Sociology, History, Government, and Humanities.
- Agreement made with 'Student Life and Affairs' office to sponsor 2 entertainment programs each semester to focus on African American Culture.

March, 2013
Task 2 – Brand the program and select the college in which it will be housed
The following month produced a home for the new home and brand for the program. The logistics for supporting the program are in place, as well as a small marketing strategy to recruit students.

- Agreement was reached to house the African American Studies program in the College of Humanities.
- Professional Support Staff have been hired to schedule and input the courses in DataCall to be available in the online schedule of courses.
- The college communications and graphics department have branded the program. The following promotional materials have been created: pamphlets, posters, course flyers, and bulletin boards [2] to be placed in high traffic areas on campus.

Figure: 7.2 Business Progress Report   Spacing and formatting requirements

continued on next page

Work Remaining
Task 3 – Obtain District Approvals and Articulation Agreements
We will need to concentrate on getting approvals of the emphasis degree and the certificate of study for those students who wish to have documentation on their transcripts while holding degrees in other disciplines such as Business Management. The scenario would be: Bachelor of Business Management with certification in African American Studies. The following need to happen.

(10)

- The District Curriculum Committee will need to approve the emphasis degree in African American studies.
- The certificate in African American Studies will need to be approved by the District Curriculum Committee.
- Research Articulation Agreements with other universities: Lawton University, The State University of Texas, and the West Texas State.

At this time, the establishment of the African American Studies program is on schedule. The steering committee understands that the program must be launched fall 2013. We have all indications that the degree and certification approvals will come to fruition. We have also begun conversations on articulation with department chairs on our targeted institutions.

Figure: 7.2 Business Progress Report   Spacing and formatting requirements

NOTES

Legend

1. **Claim** – A clear statement denoting the completion date for the formation of a new academic program. The writer is making a claim that the project will in fact be completed on this date.
2. **Support** – This is evidence that supports the claim which contends that the program will be up and running by May 15, 2013.
3. **Support** – Further evidence that the deadline will be met.
4. **Additional Support**
5. **Warrants** – These are the unstated beliefs that the President of the university may have. Clearly, all college Presidents want their school on the map so that they can be recognized amongst leading institutions. Warrants are assumption. The writer does not have to be a mind reader, he just needs to consider the things most important to the President with regard to a new academic program.

MEMO

To: Jerry Summers, President
             West Highland University
From: Janice Poland, Chair, African American Program
             Steering Committee
Subject: **Progress Report on the African American Studies Program**

Summary
On January 20, the president of the university authorized the creation of an African American Studies program. The projected completion date is May 15, 2013 with plans to have the program up and running fall of 2013. Thus far, we have completed Task 1 and Task 2 of the three proposed tasks.

Work Completed
February, 2013
Task 1 – Create steering committee, draft degree plan, recruit faculty
February represented a significant milestone in the creation of our new African American Studies program. A basic framework of the program was put together and will serve as a strong base from which to move forward.

- The steering committee was formed. Committee is composed of eight members that represent administration, admissions/registrar, faculty, and advisors.
- The emphasis degree has been designed by the steering committee in tandem with the Vice President of Instruction.
- Five faculty members have agreed to teach in the program to cover five disciplines: English, Sociology, History, Government, and Humanities.
- Agreement made with 'Student Life and Affairs' office to sponsor 2 entertainment programs each semester to focus on African American Culture.

February, 2013
Task 2 – Brand the program and select the college in which it will be housed
The following month produced a home for the new home and brand for the program. The logistics for supporting the program are in place, as well as a small marketing strategy to recruit students.

- Agreement was reached to house the African American Studies program in the College of Humanities.
- Professional Support Staff have been hired to schedule and input the courses in DataCall to be available in the online schedule of courses.
- The college communications and graphics department have branded the program. The following promotional materials have been created: pamphlets, posters, course flyers, and bulletin boards [2] to be placed in high traffic areas on campus.

Figure: 7.3 Business Progress Report   Focuses on Toulmin Elements

continued on next page

Work Remaining
Task 3 – Obtain District Approvals and Articulation Agreements
We will need to concentrate on getting approvals of the emphasis degree and the certificate of study for those students who wish to have documentation on their transcripts while holding degrees in other disciplines such as Business Management. The scenario would be: Bachelor of Business Management with certification in African American Studies. The following need to happen.

- The District Curriculum Committee will need to approve the emphasis degree in African American studies.
- The certificate in African American Studies will need to be approved by the District Curriculum Committee.
- Research Articulation Agreements with other universities: Lawton University, The State University of Texas, and the West Texas State.

At this time, the establishment of the African American Studies program is on schedule. This new academic program will enhance the standing of our university nationally. We will be among five universities in the top twenty-five in the nation that offers a degree in African American studies. We will be the only institution that offers a certification in African American Studies which can be paired with other degrees. The steering committee understands that the program must be launched fall 2013. We have all indications that the degree and certification approvals will come to fruition. We have also begun conversations on articulation with department chairs on our targeted institutions.

Figure: 7.3 Business Progress Report   Focuses on Toulmin Elements

Progress Report – Term Paper

To: Dr. Ralph McKinnon, Graduate Advisor
From: Barbara Lewis
Date: April 12, 2013

Subject: **The Use of Western Rhetorical Devices in
           Eastern Sacred Texts**

Project Overview:
For my term project, I plan to write a paper that will demonstrate the use of western rhetorical devices in eastern sacred texts. Understandably, western rhetorical theory was written to analyze western texts only. At this time, there have been no attempts to complete a cross-cultural application. The successful completion of this project will launch a new approach in the application of rhetorical theory. This project will also demonstrate the commonalities between eastern and western texts.

Work Completed

January 12:   Started research on the primary text, the Hindu Upanishads. My goal is to read a scholarly translation of the text.

February 17: Finished reading and studying the Upanishads. Began reviewing the work of my primary theorist, Kenneth Burke. I have decided to use his concept of 'identification' as a means to analyze the Hindu texts. Scheduled an interview with Dr. George Baker, the university's authority on Kenneth Burk.

February 26: Started researching scholarly articles that analyze the Upanishads as records of individual paths to enlightenment. Interviewed Yogi Ramasara for additional commentary on these texts.

March 17:   Interviewed Dr. Henry Vessel, Professor of Religious Studies for a western perspective of the texts.

Work in Progress
At this time, I have begun drafting a rough outline of my paper. I have completed the introduction, the section that will explain Burke's theory of identification, and the section which will serve as an overview of the Upanishads.

Figure: 7.4 Term Project Progress Report

continued on next page

Work to be Completed

April 18:   Finish writing the paper, proofread, and prepare the
                 bibliography.

April 20:   Scheduled Dr. Vessel to 'read through' the paper for any
                 inconsistencies.

Completion Date: May 4, 2013

Complications and Successes:
The best translations of the Upanishads are difficult to obtain. Hence, I have
had to rely on Commentaries outside the mainstream. However, my primary text is considered one of the best in the field of eastern religions. This
combined with my strong analytical skills, background in religious studies,
and a sound understanding of Burke's theory of 'identification' has put me in
an excellent position to write a successful paper. I look forward to defending
my work.

Figure: 7.4 Term Project Progress Report

NOTES

Legend

1. Single space the heading.
2. 1 line space above and below subject line.
3. 1 line space between the subject line and the opening paragraph.
4. Single spaced paragraphs throughout.
5. 1 line space above and below the 'Work Completed' line.
6. 1 line space between the 'work completed' line and the first entry.
7. 1 line space between all single spaces entries.
8. Make sure the entries are aligned on the left.
9. Make sure your dates are aligned on the right.
10. 1 line space
11. 1 line space
12. 1 line space
13. 1 line space between entries
14. 1 line space

Progress Report – Term Paper

To: Dr. Ralph McKinnon, Graduate Advisor
From: Barbara Lewis
Date: April 12, 2013

Subject: **The Use of Western Rhetorical Devices in
               Eastern Sacred Texts**

Project Overview:
For my term project, I plan to write a paper that will demonstrate the use
of western rhetorical devices in eastern sacred texts. Understandably, western rhetorical theory was written to analyze western texts only. At this
time, there have been no attempts to complete a cross-cultural application.
The successful completion of this project will launch a new approach in
the application of rhetorical theory. This project will also demonstrate the
commonalities between eastern and western texts.

Work Completed

January 12:   Started research on the primary text, the Hindu Upanishads.
                    My goal is to read a scholarly translation of the text.

February 17:   Finished reading and studying the Upanishads. Began
                    reviewing the work of my primary theorist, Kenneth Burke.
                    I have decided to use his concept of 'identification' as a means
                    to analyze the Hindu texts. Scheduled an interview with Dr
                    George Baker, the university's authority on Kenneth Burk.

February 26:   Started researching scholarly articles that analyze the
                    Upanishads as records of individual paths to enlightenment.
                    Interviewed Yogi Ramasara for additional commentary on
                    these texts.

March 17:   Interviewed Dr. Henry Vessel, Professor of Religious Studies
                    for a western perspective of the texts.

Work in Progress
At this time, I have begun drafting a rough outline of my paper. I have
completed the introduction, the section that will explain Burke's theory
of identification, and the section which will serve as an overview of the
Upanishads.

Figure: 7.5 Term Project Progress Report   Formatting and Spacing Requirements

continued on next page

(11)   **Work to be Completed**
April 18:   Finish writing the paper, proofread, and prepare the
                 bibliography.

(12)   April 20:   Scheduled Dr. Vessel to 'read through' the paper for any
                 inconsistencies.

(13)   **Completion Date:** May 4, 2013

(14)   **Complications and Successes:**
The best translations of the Upanishads are difficult to obtain. Hence, I
have had to rely on Commentaries outside the mainstream. However, my
primary text is considered one of the best in the field of eastern religions.
This combined with my strong analytical skills, background in religious
studies, and a sound understanding of Burke's theory of 'identification' has
put me in an excellent position to write a successful paper. I look forward
to defending my work.

Figure: 7.5 Term Project Progress Report   Formatting and Spacing Requirements

NOTES

Legend

1. **Claim** – writer clearly states what he intends to do.
2. **Warrants** – The writer is addressing what he thinks his professor feels is most important in academics. This would be an unstated belief the professor might have.
3. **Support** – All of the work thus far is evidence that a high quality paper will be completed. There is a sure progression toward an intended goal.
4. **Additional Support** – pointing to a successful completion of the project. Thus the initial Claim has been supported by strong evidence.
5. **Warrants** – These are more unstated beliefs that may be held in the mind of the graduate advisor. All professors worry about quality of a students project. Here, the writer is acknowledging some weak points, but quickly points out the fact that his skills and background will deliver a successful paper.

Progress Report – Term Paper

To: Dr. Ralph McKinnon, Graduate Advisor
From: Barbara Lewis
Date: April 12, 2013

Subject: **The Use of Western Rhetorical Devices in Eastern Sacred Texts**

Project Overview:
For my term project, I plan to write a paper that will demonstrate the use of western rhetorical devices in eastern sacred texts. Understandably, western rhetorical theory was written to analyze western texts only. At this time, there have been no attempts to complete a cross-cultural application. The successful completion of this project will launch a new approach in the application of rhetorical theory. This project will also demonstrate the commonalities between eastern and western texts.

Work Completed

January 12:   Started research on the primary text, the Hindu Upanishads. My goal is to read a scholarly translation of the text.

February 17:   Finished reading and studying the Upanishads. Began reviewing the work of my primary theorist, Kenneth Burke. I have decided to use his concept of 'identification' as a means to analyze the Hindu texts. Scheduled an interview with Dr. George Baker, the university's authority on Kenneth Burke.

February 26:   Started researching scholarly articles that analyze the Upanishads as records of individual paths to enlightenment. Interviewed Yogi Ramasara for additional commentary on these texts.

March 17:   Interviewed Dr. Henry Vessel, Professor of Religious Studies for a western perspective of the texts.

Work in Progress
At this time, I have begun drafting a rough outline of my paper. I have completed the introduction, the section that will explain Burke's theory of identification, and the section which will serve as an overview of the Upanishads.

Figure: 7.6 Term Project Progress Report   Shows the placement of Toulmin Elements

continued on next page

④— **Work to be Completed**

April 18:   Finish writing the paper, proofread, and prepare the bibliography.

April 20:   Scheduled Dr. Vessel to 'read through' the paper for any inconsistencies.

Completion Date: May 4, 2013

Complications and Successes:

⑤— The best translations of the Upanishads are difficult to obtain. Hence, I have had to rely on Commentaries outside the mainstream. However, my primary text is considered one of the best in the field of eastern religions. This combined with my strong analytical skills, background in religious studies, and a sound understanding of Burke's theory of 'identification' has put me in an excellent position to write a successful paper. I look forward to defending my work.

Figure: 7.6 Term Project Progress Report   Shows the placement of Toulmin Elements

MEMORANDUM

Date: July 7, 2012
To: Stephen Barton, V.P. Operations
From: Lindsey Rawlins, Corporate Human Resources Director

Subject: **Events for Launching the Wellness Program**

Overview:

For the past two months, I developed a series of events to launch a new company program. The new wellness program will be part of professional development. The purpose of the wellness program is to promote good health by encouraging daily exercise and a sensible diet. The wellness program is built on the concept that mind, body, and health are reciprocal. Thus, a healthy body gives way to a sharp mind. A sharp mind is a productive mind. And productive minds company wide yield higher profits.

Events Hosted

I have hosted three department meetings to explain the program as well as the resulting implications. The first event was a joint endeavor that included three administrative departments: accounting, customer service, and order/billing. It took place on June 3. The second event took place on June 6 in the distribution center. The third even took place on June 8 in the production facility. These meetings were designed to promote the concept of mind, body, and health and to show how attention to this is a benefit to the individual and the company. The agenda for each meeting included an explanation of the program by me, and a brief talk from the training director to explain how it will be considered professional development. Lunch was also catered.

External Marketing

In addition to hosting company meetings, I have met with the local print and television media concerns to gain some exposure in the community. On June 12, I met with the community news manager at KBLT-TV to discuss some possible air time. On June 23, I met with the editor of the local news for the Benton Times Herald.

Seminars Attended

On June 30, I attended a local wellness event hosted by Johnson College. A seminar on mind, body, health was paneled by Dr. James White of Sinai Hospital, Jane Smith, RN of the Crosby Aerobics Center, and Jill Smithson, Ph.D., the managing director of Natural Fitness, Incorporated.

Benefits

My strategy to launch the wellness program both at the company and in the community will go far in improving the image of JBP Enterprises. It will position US as a partner with the community in promoting good health. Because there will be free medical screenings and preventative healthy seminars, our employees will be able to see the advantages in the short term and the long term.

Figure: 7.7 Periodic Activity Report - Read Only Version

Legend

1. *Claim* – The purpose of the program is too promote employee and company health which is also the claim. This writer claims the new program will be beneficial to the company.
2. *Support* – Each of these categories of activities is evidence of the writer's activities that support his claim that there will be a successful launch both company wide and for the community.
3. *Warrants* – The writer assumes his vice-president is bottom line driven. Hence, he writes about the benefits of the new program which will be good for the company and the community. Remember, warrants constitute audience analysis. A writer must get into the 'head' of his audience and write to address their beliefs or concerns in a positive manner.

MEMORANDUM

Date: July 7, 2012
To: Stephen Barton, V.P. Operations
From: Lindsey Rawlins, Corporate Human Resources Director

Subject: **Events for Launching the Wellness Program**

Overview:
For the past two months, I developed a series of events to launch a new company program. The new wellness program will be part of professional development. The purpose of the wellness program is to promote good health by encouraging daily exercise and a sensible diet. The wellness program is built on the concept that mind, body, and health are reciprocal. Thus, a healthy body gives way to a sharp mind. A sharp mind is a productive mind. And productive minds company wide yield higher profits.

Events Hosted
I have hosted three department meetings to explain the program as well as the resulting implications. The first event was a joint endeavor that included three administrative departments: accounting, customer service, and order/billing. It took place on June 3. The second event took place on June 6 in the distribution center. The third even took place on June 8 in the production facility. These meetings were designed to promote the concept of mind, body, and health and to show how attention to this is a benefit to the individual and the company. The agenda for each meeting included an explanation of the program by me, and a brief talk from the training director to explain how it will be considered professional development. Lunch was also catered.

External Marketing
In addition to hosting company meetings, I have met with the local print and television media concerns to gain some exposure in the community. On June 12, I met with the community news manager at KBLT-TV to discuss some possible air time. On June 23, I met with the editor of the local news for the Benton Times Herald.

Seminars Attended
On June 30, I attended a local wellness event hosted by Johnson College. A seminar on mind, body, health was paneled by Dr. James White of Sinai Hospital, Jane Smith, RN of the Crosby Aerobics Center, and Jill Smithson, Ph.D., the managing director of Natural Fitness, Incorporated.

Benefits
My strategy to launch the wellness program both at the company and in the community will go far in improving the image of JBP Enterprises. It will position US as a partner with the community in promoting good health. Because there will be free medical screenings and preventative healthy seminars, our employees will be able to see the advantages in the short term and the long term.

Figure: 7.8 Periodic Activity Report   Shows placement of Toulmin Elements

NOTES

To: Dr. Mary Potter, V.P Instruction
From: Jane Arlington, Dean, Developmental Studies
Date: March 18, 2013

Subject: The Feasibility of Hiring Additional Development Writing Faculty

BACKGROUND
In the February 3 department meeting, we discussed the need to hire additional developmental writing faculty because of the NAAC rules. The proportion of full-time faculty to part-time faculty is in violation. As a result, it is becoming increasingly difficult to ensure consistency in the developmental writing program. As you requested, I have compiled some information that should justify the additional hires.

RECOMMENDATION
We should approach this problem on three fronts. These are our options: hire additional full time faculty, conduct a program review, and establish evaluation procedures for part-time faculty. This will secure our standing in the NAAC and enrich our department.

Rationale
The National Association of Accredited Colleges stipulates 70% of faculty should be full-time and 30% should be part-time. If this ratio is not adhered too, our college will loose its standing. Additionally, the grade distribution in the developmental writing program is falling. The academic year 2010-2012 saw a decrease across the board in the A, B, and C range. The number of A's fell 10%. The number of B's fell 8%. And the number of C's fell 5%.

ALTERNATIVES

1. Hire additional faculty and conduct a program review or,
2. do not hire additional faculty and do not conduct a program review.

SUGGESTED ACTION
In order to maintain our accreditation, overhaul the writing program, and improve grade distribution, the following action items are viable:

- Hire 3 full time developmental faculty members.
- Hire 2 full time visiting scholars with 2 year contracts.
- Create a program review committee.
- Appoint a lead faculty member to coordinate yearly evaluations of all adjunct instructors.

OVERALL FEASIBILITY
The simplest way to approach our problem is to adopt the action items. Without additional faculty, a program review, and an evaluation process for part-time faculty, we will not be able to meet NAAC policy, redesign our program and ensure its future success. This will provide an immediate solution to the problem. It will also be a much needed investment in the future of this department, our institution, and our students.

Figure: 7.9 Feasibility Report - Read Only Version

Legend

1. Single space the heading
2. 1 line space above and below the subject line.
3. Always use the provided side-headings. Always type them in 'caps' and 'bold'
4. 1 line space between the sections.
5. Side Heading – Caps and Bold
6. Always single-space the paragraphs
7. Side Heading – Caps and Bold
8. Side Heading – Caps and Bold
9. Bullets are acceptable if space is not an issue, but not required. Manage your page space carefully. Try to keep to one page.
10. Side heading – Caps and Bold. No line space between the 'overall feasibility' and suggested action sections

To: Dr. Mary Potter, V.P Instruction
From: Jane Arlington, Dean, Developmental Studies
Date: March 18, 2013

Subject: The Feasibility of Hiring Additional Development Writing Faculty

BACKGROUND
In the February 3 department meeting, we discussed the need to hire additional developmental writing faculty because of the NAAC rules. The proportion of full-time faculty to part-time faculty is in violation. As a result, it is becoming increasingly difficult to ensure consistency in the developmental writing program. As you requested, I have compiled some information that should justify the additional hires.

RECOMMENDATION
We should approach this problem on three fronts. These are our options: hire additional full time faculty, conduct a program review, and establish evaluation procedures for part-time faculty. This will secure our standing in the NAAC and enrich our department.

Rationale
The National Association of Accredited Colleges stipulates 70% of faculty should be full-time and 30% should be part-time. If this ratio is not adhered too, our college will loose its standing. Additionally, the grade distribution in the developmental writing program is falling. The academic year 2010-2012 saw a decrease across the board in the A, B, and C range. The number of A's fell 10%. The number of B's fell 8%. And the number of C's fell 5%.

ALTERNATIVES
1. Hire additional faculty and conduct a program review or,
2. do not hire additional faculty and do not conduct a program review.

SUGGESTED ACTION
In order to maintain our accreditation, overhaul the writing program, and improve grade distribution, the following action items are viable:

- Hire 3 full time developmental faculty members.
- Hire 2 full time visiting scholars with 2 year contracts.
- Create a program review committee.
- Appoint a lead faculty member to coordinate yearly evaluations of all adjunct instructors.

OVERALL FEASIBILITY
The simplest way to approach our problem is to adopt the action items. Without additional faculty, a program review, and an evaluation process for part-time faculty, we will not be able to meet NAAC policy, redesign our program and ensure its future success. This will provide an immediate solution to the problem. It will also be a much needed investment in the future of this department, our institution, and our students.

Figure: 7.10 Feasibility Report Spacing/Format Requirements

Legend

1. **Warrants** – In this case, warrants are easily discovered. There have been stated beliefs rather than unstated beliefs. The writer has already been made aware of the vice-president's concerns and can tailor the argument to those.
2. **Claim** – This recommendation is a clearly stated claim. Hire additional faculty, conduct a program review, and evaluate part time faculty. The feasibility of this claim will be argued with the following support.
3. **Support** – By providing a reasons why action should be taken, the writer begins to build support for the feasibility of the claim.
4. **Support** – This is further support that argues the feasibility of the claim.
5. **Warrants** – The writer continues to address the warrants of his vice president which is in this case, some interior fears. He points to the down side of what could happen if they do nothing. And then points to a bright future if his claim is accepted as feasible.

To: Dr. Mary Potter, V.P Instruction
From: Jane Arlington, Dean, Developmental Studies
Date: March 18, 2013

Subject: The Feasibility of Hiring Additional Development Writing Faculty

BACKGROUND
In the February 3 department meeting, we discussed the need to hire additional developmental writing faculty because of the NAAC rules. The proportion of full-time faculty to part-time faculty is in violation. As a result, it is becoming increasingly difficult to ensure consistency in the developmental writing program. As you requested, I have compiled some information that should justify the additional hires.

RECOMMENDATION
We should approach this problem on three fronts. These are our options: hire additional full time faculty, conduct a program review, and establish evaluation procedures for part-time faculty. This will secure our standing in the NAAC and enrich our department.

Rationale
The National Association of Accredited Colleges stipulates 70% of faculty should be full-time and 30% should be part-time. If this ratio is not adhered too, our college will loose its standing. Additionally, the grade distribution in the developmental writing program is falling. The academic year 2010-2012 saw a decrease across the board in the A, B, and C range. The number of A's fell 10%. The number of B's fell 8%. And the number of C's fell 5%.

ALTERNATIVES

1. Hire additional faculty and conduct a program review or,
2. do not hire additional faculty and do not conduct a program review.

SUGGESTED ACTION
In order to maintain our accreditation, overhaul the writing program, and improve grade distribution, the following action items are viable:

- Hire 3 full time developmental faculty members.
- Hire 2 full time visiting scholars with 2 year contracts.
- Create a program review committee.
- Appoint a lead faculty member to coordinate yearly evaluations of all adjunct instructors.

OVERALL FEASIBILITY
The simplest way to approach our problem is to adopt the action items. Without additional faculty, a program review, and an evaluation process for part-time faculty, we will not be able to meet NAAC policy, redesign our program and ensure its future success. This will provide an immediate solution to the problem. It will also be a much needed investment in the future of this department, our institution, and our students.

Figure: 7.11 Feasibility Report   Toulmin Highlights

NOTES

Minutes for Human Resources Meeting
July 10, 2013 – 2:00 p m

Type of Meeting: Bi-Weekly – Status – Training Managers

Meeting Called By: Linda Burk, Human Resource Director

Note Taker: Randy Baker

Members Present: Louis Williams, Jonas Gimlet, Alice Johnson, Randy Baker, Christine Minor, Paula Michaels

Agenda Topics:
   Call to Order Meeting was called to order by Linda Burk on Tuesday, 2:00 p.m. July 10.

   Approval of the Minutes The minutes for the previous meeting on July 2, meetings were read. There were no corrections made.

   New Business Linda announced new professional development modules for administrative support.

   - The first group of modules will begin August 1, 2012.
   - Completion of these modules will be included in the employee's yearly evaluation.
   - There will be three modules: global workplace communication, global ethics in the workplace, team building in a diverse environment.
   - Each of these modules must be completed before the employee's yearly evaluation.

   Discussion Items

   - Christine Minor requested a demonstration of the modules by the firm who designed them. She felt it necessary that the trainers be trained by those who had created the product.
   - Alice Johnson needed clarification on the announcement and scheduling of these modules. She also discussed the impact of assessment with regard to an employee's overall evaluation.
   - Jonus was interested in the module selections. He asked Linda to review the process asking: What is the overall long term purpose of these types of modules? Who in corporate originated the idea of training for global awareness. How the specific models were selected?

   Action Items None were assigned to any members

Adjournment: Meeting was adjourned at 3:30 p.m.

Figure: 7.12 Meeting Minutes - Read Only Version

Legend

1. *All Side headings should be positioned against the left margin. The margin default should be 1 inch.*
2. Side Heading
3. There should be 1 line space between all Side-Headings.
4. Side Heading
5. Side Heading
6. Side Heading
7. Agenda items should be 1 tab space from the left margin.
8. Keep Agenda items 1 tab space to the right of the left margin.
9. Keep Discussion Items 1 tab space from left margin. It should be aligned with previous agenda topics.
10. Action Items should be indented 1 tab space from the left margin to align with the previous agenda items.
11. Side Heading – Keep against the left margin. Aligned with other side headings.

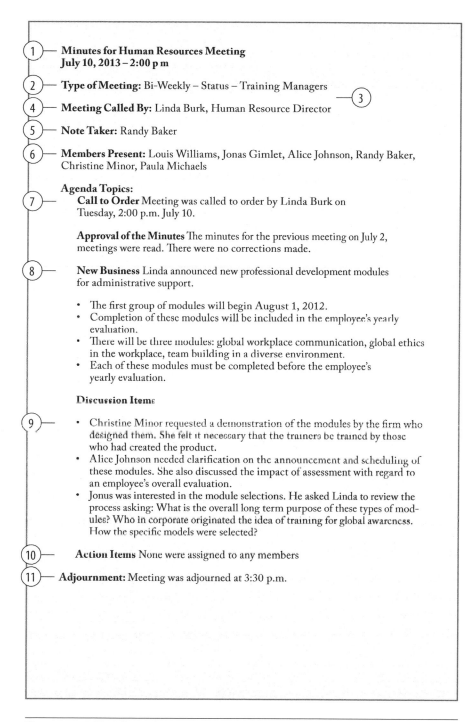

① — **Minutes for Human Resources Meeting**
July 10, 2013 – 2:00 p m

② — **Type of Meeting:** Bi-Weekly – Status – Training Managers ③

④ — **Meeting Called By:** Linda Burk, Human Resource Director

⑤ — **Note Taker:** Randy Baker

⑥ — **Members Present:** Louis Williams, Jonas Gimlet, Alice Johnson, Randy Baker, Christine Minor, Paula Michaels

Agenda Topics:

⑦ — **Call to Order** Meeting was called to order by Linda Burk on Tuesday, 2:00 p.m. July 10.

Approval of the Minutes The minutes for the previous meeting on July 2, meetings were read. There were no corrections made.

⑧ — **New Business** Linda announced new professional development modules for administrative support.

- The first group of modules will begin August 1, 2012.
- Completion of these modules will be included in the employee's yearly evaluation.
- There will be three modules: global workplace communication, global ethics in the workplace, team building in a diverse environment.
- Each of these modules must be completed before the employee's yearly evaluation.

Discussion Items

⑨ —
- Christine Minor requested a demonstration of the modules by the firm who designed them. She felt it necessary that the trainers be trained by those who had created the product.
- Alice Johnson needed clarification on the announcement and scheduling of these modules. She also discussed the impact of assessment with regard to an employee's overall evaluation.
- Jonus was interested in the module selections. He asked Linda to review the process asking: What is the overall long term purpose of these types of modules? Who in corporate originated the idea of training for global awareness. How the specific models were selected?

⑩ — **Action Items** None were assigned to any members

⑪ — **Adjournment:** Meeting was adjourned at 3:30 p.m.

Figure: 7.13 Meeting Minutes With Spacing requirements

EXERCISES

1. Think about problems to be solved or processes to be improved. If you currently hold a job, write a progress report to your manager explaining the progress you have made on a recent project.

2. If you are currently a student, write a progress report for a term project in which you describe the progress you've made so far.

3. If you are either a current student, or holding a job, write a periodic activity report that describes the details of a project you have been involved with over time.

4. Write a feasibility report on **one** of the following options:

   *You are trying to buy a car. You have narrowed your search to **two** 'models'. Write a feasibility report that determines the best vehicle for you.*

   You are currently on a job. There are three situations that require – attention around the office: purchases of new equipment, additional hires, or changes in work schedules. Pick one and write a feasibility report that will advise your manager which course to take.

WHY IS IT IMPORTANT?.... CONVINCE ME ALREADY!

PROPOSALS AND THE EXECUTIVE SUMMARY

WHAT TYPE OF PROPOSAL SHOULD I EXPECT TO WRITE?

Generally, large companies or corporations have entire departments staffed with professional proposal writers. This section will look at two types of proposals you will likely write as a conscientious employee that sees areas in which change can affect the productivity of your department. These types of proposals are: an internal proposal and an external proposal. You will be provided illustrations of an internal proposal to study at the end of this section because this is the one you will most likely write often.

WHAT ARE THEY EXACTLY?

What's a proposal? They come in various shapes and sizes. They can be either internal or external. They can be either solicited or unsolicited. They can be as short as an email and as long as a ten page document. They are always persuasive in nature. In short, proposals are arguments. And as you know by now, the Toulmin Model is a means by which to write persuasive business documents that do exactly that, argue toward a planned goal.

253

SHAPES AND SIZES

All proposals have PMB – Purpose-Message-Benefit

Internal Proposal The **purpose** of an internal proposal will be to persuade your boss or supervisor to:

- change a process
- solve a problem
- purchase products, services or pursue activities
- conduct research or make changes in policies

All of these should benefit the company in some way.

The **message** will always be persuasive, fact based, and verifiable. The **benefit** can come in the form of improvements in productivity and profitability and will likely contribute to another accomplishment line on your resume.

Solicited or Unsolicited, Which One Will Be My Greatest Advantage?

Both can work for you in different ways.

- *The Unsolicited Internal Proposal* – These are proposals that have not been requested by a manager. These types of proposals are opportunities to cast you as a proactive, forward thinking employee. This is your time to boost your image. For example, suppose you realize that the office network's current operations system slows down the production of sales orders. Changing operating systems would increase productivity. You write a memo describing what is going on, what you want to do, why you want to do it, what it will cost and what will be the overall benefit. This is an unsolicited internal proposal is a means to sell your creative ideas.
- *A Solicited Internal Proposal* – These proposals are requested by a manager or supervisor. There may not be a need for you come up with 'the answer' or solve the problem. Your boss may have already provided the solution and simply requests you measure its viability. This is still an opportunity for you to gain some good exposure because you will have to use your critical thinking skills and make a recommendation.

External Proposal The **purpose** of an external proposal is to seek prospective suppliers to bid on business that the company cannot provide for itself:

- unusual expertise in areas not already provided within the company
- new products

- market research
- analytical reports
- special services

The **message** in an external proposal will not necessarily be persuasive. It will be a special request for information or products and services. These requests can come in the form of a bid for standard products or services, or it can request products or services that are more specialized such as a new product design, packaging, or special delivery systems.

The **benefit** is obvious: new products and/or services that will improve the company's bottom line or productivity.

External proposals are usually solicited. From the potential supplier/vendor's point of view, they are being approached to offer services.

WRITING A PROPOSAL FOR WORK

What not to Expect

First, do not expect to write formal proposals unless you have been hired specifically to serve on a proposal team. These proposals are comprehensive, well researched documents that can be ten or more pages. Corporations have entire departments staffed with professional proposal writers to create these

What to Expect

The type of proposal you more than likely find yourself writing will be *an internal unsolicited proposal discussed earlier.* It will be in the form of a medium length email or a memo. Remember, this informal proposal does not have to be written on the level of a formal proposal written by professional proposal writer. It should not exceed more than two pages if presented as a memo, and no more than a six paragraph email.

Expect it to be persuasive It will need to convince your manager or supervisor that your ideas will work. In a nutshell, the benefits produced will far outweigh the costs of implementation. Your manager will need to believe that:

- you fully understand the organization's mission: productive, profitable, and innovative
- you fully understand the organization's operations
- you fully understand the necessity of the proposal
- you know the solution
- you know how to implement the solution

Expect it to be Persuasive Expect to use all or most of the six elements. In previous sections, the basic three were always needed: claim, support, and warrants. These earlier documents such as reports, workplace letters, email, memos and job application letters were intended to be much shorter and less intense in terms of basic argument strategy. These documents needed to make their claim known early, state the most concise support, include some brief warrants. In short, they need to 'wrap it up' as quickly as possible.

Internal Proposals will need to be more strategically mapped out because you will need to create an argument that will also present the counter-argument, *the rebuttal*. You will need to use the rebuttal because internal proposals must always include a cost-benefit section. This is your counter argument that will way lay cost implications. The mandatory three elements required in earlier documents become the mandatory four elements in internal proposals. They **must be** used.

Other elements that **may be** strategically used are backing and qualifiers. If you remember, 'backing' is additional warrants. In internal proposals, qualifiers give you some wiggle room in your proposed solutions or improvements. Simply put, think of qualifiers as qualifying language.

For example, do not state: This proposed solution will *undoubtedly yield* positive results. It locks you into a certain outcome that might not be met, thus putting you in a negative light. Instead, use qualifying language: This proposed solution will *more than likely* yield positive results. This type of phrasing will not lock you into a certain outcome. You will have the room to either be successful or not successful without doing yourself great harm.

Mandatory Toulmin: 4 Elements that Must be Included

- claim
- support
- warrants
- rebuttal

Optional Toulmin: 2 Elements that May be Included

- backing
- qualifiers

SECTIONS OF AN INTERNAL PROPOSAL

Your boss or supervisor will expect an easy-to-read, clear presentation that is informative and covers all the bases. Therefore, plan on including to the list of sections below:

- Subject Line
- Background
- Statement of the Problem
- Proposed Solution
- Proposed Plan
- Costs
- Benefits
- Conclusion

STRUCTURE OF AN INTERNAL PROPOSAL: 8 Essential Features
What You Should Write. How You Should Write. And Toulmin, of course!

The structure of a proposal consists of several essential features or sections. The Toulmin Model should be embedded in these sections with the exception of the 'subject line.' The subject line has a unique purpose outside Toulmin by acting as a title and attention getter. After this section, you will have three illustrations to study: a read only version, a Toulmin highlighted version, and a formatting version.

1. **Subject Line**
   Your subject line should act as a 'title' for your proposal. It should be specific and not overly generalized. It is persuasive in this sense: do not be vague. Your manager needs to be persuaded to read your proposal. The best chance for this is to make sure your intent is clear and focused. An example of over-generalization would be: 'A Proposal for Changing Office Procedures'. To be more specific, try: 'A Proposal for Streamlining the Order-Billing Process.'

2. **Background**
   Think of 'background' as context, the environment in which you work. It may not always be perfect and operate with 100% efficiency. Do not assume your boss understands all of the details contributing to a particular issue that needs to be resolved. You must relay this information succinctly but with as much detail as

you can provide. Your manager needs to have a clear picture of events leading up to the problem, anything or anyone that may be affected by the problem, and any negative consequences resulting from a lack of action.

WARRANTS and BACKING – You will need to address the unstated questions and concerns of your bosses. This area is basically audience psychology. Put yourself in your 'boss's shoes.' Fill in any blanks in information he or she may have. 'Backing' is considered additional warrants.

3. **Statement of the Problem**
   This section is a follow up to the 'background.' You have created a setting and given details of how the problem was created and possible affects. Now you must state the problem clearly and concisely. Try to keep it to three to four sentences. Remember, this informal proposal should not exceed more than two pages if presented as a memo, and no more than a six paragraph email.

   WARRANTS – You are stating the problem, but you must also continue to address audience warrants. Your boss will undeniably want a problem free workplace, an unstated belief. You must convince him that this problem is real and demands action.

4. **Proposed Solution**
   Briefly describe the solution and explain why it is feasible. That is, explain why the solution is achievable, practical, and appropriate? This should not exceed three to four sentences or a 150 word paragraph.

   CLAIM – Your proposed solution is your claim. The opening sentence in this section should be a clear and straightforward sentence that presents a solution. Continue writing this area in a confident tone that will convey credibility

5. **Proposed Plan**
   This is where you state the details of what must be done to solve the problem. You will also need to be specific in terms of what you will so, why you will do it, and how it will be carried out. Use language that does not guarantee absolutes.

   SUPPORT and QUALIFIERS – Your proposed plan supports the claim and should use qualifying language that does not guarantee absolutes. Unforeseen circumstances may come into play

6. Costs

This section describes the costs of your solution. You may set it up in line items, or a budget table. Your boss should have a clear idea of how much it will cost to implement your proposed solution.

REBUTTAL – Consider this section your rebuttal. It is the counter argument with regard to financial costs. Write to persuade the reader of the feasibility and advantages of making the investment. This should ease concerns of budgetary conflicts.

7. Benefits

This is where you explain what stands to be gained if your proposed solution is implemented. Here, you can list all of the specific improvements that will take place.

WARRANTS are found in the benefits and conclusion. You are addressing the unstated concerns of your audience. You are also addressing possible negatives with positives as you conclude the proposal.

8. Conclusion

This area reaffirms the need for the proposal and calls for action. It should have a confident tone and end with an optimistic vision for the future.

GUIDELINES for Persuasive Proposals

- **MAKE SURE** you choose a suitable format for delivery. If you are writing an internal proposal whether unsolicited or solicited, choose either email or memo. If you are writing an external memo, use a standard document format with default setting. Be sure to include a cover letter, title page, and table of contents.
- **MAKE SURE** your **subject line** [internal proposal] or **title** [external proposal] is clear and brief so that the readers will know exactly what to expect.
- **MAKE SURE** you compose your **background** keeping **warrants** in mind. Address questions you think your boss will raise with regard to the context of the problem.
- **MAKE SURE** you **state your problem** and **use warrants** effectively. Remember that your superiors want a smooth running problem free workplace. State your problem so that they understand why your proposal is so important.

- **MAKE SURE** you present the **proposed solution** quickly as you write this section. Your solution is a recommendation. **This is your claim** which must be argued successfully. Keep warrants in mind.
- **MAKE SURE** you write the **proposed plan** much like the **support** in any other argument. It is the evidence that will persuade your boss to accept your proposal. He or she will want need to believe that your solution will work.
- **MAKE SURE** you address as many objections as you can in the **cost** area. This is your **rebuttal** or counter-argument to the attitude, "it's too expensive to fix."
- **MAKE SURE** your **benefits** outweigh the costs. Your boss should be convinced that the investment is a sound one. Keep **warrants** in mind here. *Become* your boss and try to answer all of the questions he would ask you before he asks you the basic question: *How is this going to make things better given the cost?*
- **MAKE SURE** your tone is confident, informed, and optimistic.
- **MAKE SURE** your **claim is attainable**. If there are any constraints or limitations, state them. This will be when you use '**qualifiers.**' Write any potential constraints with qualifying language.
- **MAKE SURE** your **conclusion induces action.** Be sure you spell out exactly what you want them to do. Your superiors must be persuaded to '*act*' on your recommendation also known as **your claim** also known as **your proposed solution.**

MEMORANDUM

To: Loren Alcott, V.P. Operations
From: Dean Miller, Manager, Global Accounts – Export
Date: March 6, 2013

Subject: **A Proposal for Hiring Additional Staff in the Global**
Accounts – Export

Background
The global accounts team began as an experiment between the sales and
export documentation group. It has been hailed as the industry's 'new
model.' As a hybrid group that combines sales and operations, global
accounts has built a reputation as an effective partner with the Southeast
Asia sales team over the last year. Initially, global accounts was staffed
with production assistants that generated export bills of lading only.
There were no rate clerks assigned to the group. In spite of this, the team
was awarded the highest rating from quality assurance in a survey of our
multi-national clients.

Statement of the Problem
Due to this excellent rating, our multi-national client base has grown
by 8%. Export shipments have increased from one-hundred per day to
one hundred sixty per day. At this rate, our current staff will not be able
to meet this demand and retain it's A+ plus rating from quality assurance. Our reputation has been built on speedy turn times in bill of lading
production. Currently, it is one hour. Given the increase in shipments and
the lack of rate clerks, I estimate this turn time to increase to two hours.

Proposed Solution
We can increase productivity and eliminate adverse effects on turn time by
adding two additional bill of lading assistants, and two rate clerks.

Proposed Plan
Additional bill of lading assistants will address the increase in shipments.
Adding rate clerks to the global account group will decrease the amount
of time needed to complete the bill. Typically, a bill of lading must sit in a
queue twenty minutes pending rates from the respective trade lane group.
By rating our own bills, we will be able to cut the wait time in half. These
additional personnel will need to be hired and in place by the end of the
second quarter to prepare for the traditionally high volume third quarter

Figure: 8.1 Internal Unsolicited Proposal - Read Only Version

continued on next page

Costs
The major costs will be for the salaries of the additional staff. The annual salary plus benefits for a bill of lading assistant is $30,000. The annual salary and benefits for an experience rate clerk is $35,000. Minor costs will include additional work stations and computers, approximately $6,000. Total costs for four additional staff, equipment, and furniture will be $136,000.00. Even though additional staff was not included in our current budget, we will still be able to exceed our goals given the increase in productivity and shipments. Sales have projected a 16% increase in global accounts revenue for the third quarter.

Benefits
Because NTL Lines made the decision to redesign the export documentation model, global accounts has been hailed a success. This plan will protect the excellent reputation we have built with our multi-national client base. It will grow the projected annual revenue for large global accounts by 22%. It will increase productivity by 6%. And it will enrich our relationship with other stakeholders in the corporation.

Conclusion
Given the amount of exposure global accounts has received in industry trade journals as of late, an investment in additional staff is a necessity. It will solidify our place in the industry as a worldwide, world class shipping line.

Thanks

cc: Barbara Bradford, Vice-President of Finance
    Ralph Smith, Director, Corporate Human Resources
    Mitch Holden, V.P. Corporate Sales and Marketing

Figure: 8.1 Internal Unsolicited Proposal - Read Only Version

NOTES

Legend

1. This internal proposal is written in 'memo' form. Keep to 1 and ½ pages maximum. If you write in 'email' form, be aware of your length. You may want to combine sections or edit to shorten.
2. 3 line spaces between the memo line or letterhead and the heading.
3. Single space the heading. If you are using 'email' form, no heading is necessary. The fields are already provided.
4. 1 line space above and below the subject line.
5. No line spaces between the sub headings and the following paragraph.
6. 1 line space between each single spaced paragraph.
7. Single space all of the paragraphs.
8. 1 line space
9. 1 line space
10. No line space between sub heading and the paragraph.
11. You may use bullet items or tables in the cost section, or you may write in paragraph form. Let the length of your document be your guide. You do not want to exceed more than 1 and ½ pages in this internal proposal. If you choose to write this in 'email' form. Keep away from bullets and tables. Proposals via email must be kept to 4 – 5 healthy paragraphs.
12. 1 line space
13. No line spaces between the sub heading and the paragraph.
14. 1 line space above and below the closing 'thank you'
15. Single space your courtesy copy block. If this is in email form, no courtesy block is necessary. There will be fields already provided.

(1)— MEMORANDUM

(2)

To: Loren Alcott, V.P. Operations
(3)— From: Dean Miller, Manager, Global Export Documentation
Date: March 6, 2013

(4)

Subject: **A Proposal for Hiring Additional Staff in the Global
          Accounts – Export**

(5)

Background
The global accounts team began as an experiment between the sales and
export documentation group. It has been hailed as the industry's 'new
model.' As a hybrid group that combines sales and operations, global
accounts has built a reputation as an effective partner with the Southeast
Asia sales team over the last year. Initially, global accounts was staffed
with production assistants that generated export bills of lading only.
There were no rate clerks assigned to the group. In spite of this, the team
(6)— was awarded the highest rating from quality assurance in a survey of our
multi-national clients.
(7)

Statement of the Problem
Due to this excellent rating, our multi-national client base has grown
by 8%. Export shipments have increased from one-hundred per day to
one-hundred sixty per day. At this rate, our current staff will not be able
to meet this demand and retain it's A+ plus rating from quality assurance. Our reputation has been built on speedy turn times in bill of lading
production. Currently, it is one hour. Given the increase in shipments and
the lack of rate clerks, I estimate this turn time to increase to two hours.
(8)

Proposed Solution
We can increase productivity and eliminate adverse effects on turn time by
adding two additional bill of lading assistants, and two rate clerks.
(9)

Proposed Plan
(10)— Additional bill of lading assistants will address the increase in shipments.
Adding rate clerks to the global account group will decrease the amount
of time needed to complete the bill. Typically, a bill of lading must sit in a
queue twenty minutes pending rates from the respective trade lane group.
By rating our own bills, we will be able to cut the wait time in half. These
additional personnel will need to be hired and in place by the end of the
second quarter to prepare for the traditionally high volume third quarter

Figure: 8.2 Internal Unsolicited Proposal - Spacing and Formatting Requirements

continued on next page

Costs

(11) The major costs will be for the salaries of the additional staff. The annual salary plus benefits for a bill of lading assistant is $30,000. The annual salary and benefits for an experience rate clerk is $35,000. Minor costs will include additional work stations and computers, approximately $6,000. Total costs for four additional staff, equipment, and furniture will be $136,000.00. Even though additional staff was not included in our current budget, we will still be able to exceed our goals given the increase in productivity and shipments. Sales have projected a 16% increase in global accounts revenue for the third quarter.

(12)

Benefits

(13) Because NTL Lines made the decision to redesign the export documentation model, global accounts has been hailed a success. This plan will protect the excellent reputation we have built with our multi-national client base. It will grow the projected annual revenue for large global accounts by 22%. It will increase productivity by 6%. And it will enrich our relationship with other stakeholders in the corporation.

Conclusion

Given the amount of exposure global accounts has received in industry trade journals as of late, an investment in additional staff is a necessity. It will solidify our place in the industry as a worldwide, world class shipping line.

(14) Thanks

cc: Barbara Bradford, Vice-President of Finance
    Ralph Smith, Director, Corporate Human Resources
(15) Mitch Holden, V.P. Corporate Sales and Marketing

Figure: 8.2 Internal Unsolicited Proposal   Spacing and Formatting Requirements

NOTES

Legend

1. *Warrants* – Describing 'background' will address your boss's desire that your group continues to be innovative and successful. This is addressing warrants.
2. *Backing* – Backing is information that 'backs up' the warrants. You know your boss is happy to have a stellar group such as global accounts. Re affirm its success in your closing line.
3. *Warrants* – The statement of the problem is where you will address what you know your boss does not want, an unproductive workplace. His 'dislikes' are sometimes stated or unstated beliefs. Describe the problem as something that may endanger the health of the company, employees, or department. He must believe it is real and demands action.
4. *Claim* – Your proposed solution is your claim. Be sure to use precise language that implies success such as 'increase productivity.'
5. *Support* – The proposed plan is evidence of how the solution will be implemented and be successful. Remember, you are selling an idea. To sell an idea, you must provide evidence that persuades your boss to acceptance it.
6. *Qualifier* – This is qualifying language that does not make absolute guarantees. See bold words and phrasing.
7. *Rebuttal* – This constitutes your counter argument with regard to the extra expense the new hires will cause. Be sure to include evidence that points to costs being offset either tangibly or intangibly.
8. *Warrants* – More warrants in the final sections: benefits and conclusion. You must address all of the objectives and goals you believe your boss holds: profitability, productivity. In short, you must persuade him to believe this is a good investment in the future.

MEMORANDUM

To: Loren Alcott, V.P. Operations
From: Dean Miller, Manager, Global Accounts – Export
Date: March 6, 2013

Subject: **A Proposal for Hiring Additional Staff in the Global
         Accounts – Export**

Background
The global accounts team began as an experiment between the sales and export documentation group. *It has been hailed as the industry's 'new model.'* As a hybrid group that combines sales and operations, *global accounts has built a reputation as an effective partner* with the Southeast Asia sales team over the last year. Initially, global accounts was staffed with production assistants that generated export bills of lading only. There were no rate clerks assigned to the group. In spite of this, the team was awarded the highest rating from quality assurance in a survey of our multi-national clients.

Statement of the Problem
Due to this excellent rating, our multi-national client base has grown by 8%. Export shipments have increased from one-hundred per day to one-hundred sixty per day. At this rate, our current staff will not be able to meet this demand and retain its A+ plus rating from quality assurance. Our reputation has been built on speedy turn times in bill of lading production. Currently, it is one hour. Given the increase in shipments and the lack of rate clerks, I estimate this turn time to increase to two hours.

Proposed Solution
We can increase productivity and eliminate adverse effects on turn time by adding two additional bill of lading assistants, and two rate clerks.

Proposed Plan
Additional bill of lading assistants will address the increase in shipments. Adding rate clerks to the global account group will decrease the amount of time needed to complete the bill by *approximately* 35%. Typically, a bill of lading must sit in a queue twenty minutes pending rates from the respective trade lane group. By rating our own bills, *we estimate* the wait time to be cut in half. These additional personnel will need to be hired and in place by the end of the second quarter to prepare for the traditionally high volume third quarter.

Figure: 8.3 Internal Unsolicited Proposal   with Toulmin Highlights

continued on next page

Costs
The major costs will be for the salaries of the additional staff. The annual salary plus benefits for a bill of lading assistant is $30,000. The annual salary and benefits for an experience rate clerk is $35,000. Minor costs will include additional work stations and computers, approximately $6,000. Total costs for four additional staff, equipment, and furniture will be $136,000.00. Even though additional staff was not included in our current budget, we will still be able to exceed our goals given the increase in productivity and shipments. Sales have projected a 16% increase in global accounts revenue for the third quarter.

Benefits
Because NTL Lines made the decision to redesign the export documentation model, global accounts has been hailed a success. This plan will protect the excellent reputation we have built with our multi-national client base. *It will grow the projected annual revenue for large global accounts by 22%. It will increase productivity by 6%. And it will enrich our relationship with other stakeholders in the corporation.*

Conclusion
Given the amount of exposure global accounts has received in industry trade journals as of late, an investment in additional staff is a necessity. It will solidify our place in the industry as a worldwide, world class shipping line.

Thanks

cc: Barbara Bradford, Vice-President of Finance
Ralph Smith, Director, Corporate Human Resources
Mitch Holden, V.P. Corporate Sales and Marketing

Figure: 8.3 Internal Unsolicited Proposal   with Toulmin Highlights

THE EXECUTIVE SUMMARY
What is it and When Do I Use It?

Overview

An executive summary is exactly that, a summary. It's a summary of a larger argument better know as a formal proposal, the one you are least likely to write. Professional proposal writers are hired to do this. These formal proposals will and can exceed twenty pages. They may be followed by progress reports, and finally a recommendation report. Subjects of these types of formal proposals could be: product design, intranet use and utility, legal implications in company email policy, training programs for ethical conduct, outsourcing and international law.

However, this is not to say that you may not be tasked with writing a summary of this type of proposal for a busy executive. Sometimes known as a management overview or management summary, this brief document is designed to condense a large amount of information. Typically, a one-page summary will suffice for a twenty page proposal.

The executive summary should include the following sections:

- **Background** – This section must explain the background or the context, research an opportunity, identify a problem, or assess feasibility.
- **Methods** – This section describes what methods were used to investigate solutions, make inquiries, or explore possible resolutions.
- **Findings – Conclusion** – This section explains the results and conclusions that were found.
- **Recommendation** – This section offers a recommendation based on the findings and conclusions in a proposal.

THE POWER POINT – Executive Summary

Some executive summaries can be presented as a Power Point slide presentation. This is a current trend used to communicate this type of information on a different level. It is a much faster way to deliver information. It cuts to the most important points. It appeals to our 'visual nature.' The advantages of Power Point are:

- It creates an effective simultaneous print and screen presentation.
- It is a good delivery system for online meetings, webinars, and conferences/meetings.
- PP Slide shows force the writer to create concise to the point summaries that 'drill down' to the most important findings, conclusions, recommendations.
- It allows integration of charts and graphs when presenting findings.

There are two illustrations of 'print' executive summaries for you to study. One is a read only version. The other is a formatting version that highlights the required sections and spacing.

CONTENT AREAS

The content areas below are the **minimum required** and **MANDATORY**

- Introduction
- Statement of the problem
- Proposed solution
- Proposed Plan
- Costs
- Benefits
- Conclusion

Executive Summary

On April 6, 2013, Morris Jennings, Dean of Communications, directed English faculty at Carlton College to assess student retention for the academic year 2013-14. In our study, we found that there were several institutional and student based problems that contributed to decreases in retention.

Currently, Carlton College is experiencing a12% decease in retention. For the academic year 2011-12, retention was at 87%, it has dropped to 75%. Because the state's funding is tied to enrollment, it was a consensus among English faculty to create a special committee to investigate the causes that contribute to low retention levels, and provide some recommendation on how to raise retention levels to 90%.

To perform this research, we enlisted the aid of institutional research to run retention reports by discipline, gender, and ethnicity, and income. We created a survey to be distributed to composition and literature classrooms. This survey was designed to expose any inherent weaknesses in classroom methodology, financial hardships, work schedules, language barriers, and disabilities. We also created a focus group of several English faculty to discuss real-time issues in the classroom that affect student retention.

After collecting all of the data, these are the contributing factors we found:

- Lack of adequate financial aid
- Students juggling work and school
- Learning methodologies were not addressing students adequately
- The traditional 16-week term is not compatible with student completion goals
- The demand for online education is increasing due to its flexibility
- No technological innovation in classrooms

On the basis of these findings, we conclude that decreases in student retention are directly related to financial resources, incompatibility of long work hours and classroom hours, and teaching methodologies. We further recommend that the Vice-President of Instruction appoint a task force of faculty and administrators to formulate an appropriate response plan to address each of the contributing factors to low student retention.

Figure: 8.4 Read Only version of a Print Executive Summary

Legend

1. The title, Executive Summary, must be at the 1 inch top margin default. Bold the typeface.
2. 2 lines spaces between the title and the distribution line.
3. 1 line space above and below the **DISTRIBUTION LINE.**
4. All paragraphs must be single spaced.
5. Explains the **BACKGROUND**
6. Explains the **PROBLEM**
7. 1 line space between each single spaced paragraph.
8. Explains the **METHODS**
9. 1 space between the 'methods' paragraph and the 'findings' section. This section may be a list of bullets or in paragraph form.
10. **THE FINDINGS**
11. **CONCLUSION**
12. **RECOMMENDATION**
13. Printed Signature Block should include title and name of organization.
14. Courtesy Copy line.

Executive Summary —①

② To: Morris Jennings, Dean of Communications

③

④ On April 6, 2013, Morris Jennings, Dean of Communications, directed English faculty at Carlton College to assess student retention for the academic year 2013-14. In our study, we found that there were several institutional and student based problems ⑤ that contributed to decreases in retention.

Currently, Carlton College is experiencing a12% decease in retention. For the academic year 2011-12, retention was at 87%, it has dropped to 75%. Because the ⑥ state's funding is tied to enrollment, it was a consensus among English faculty to create a special committee to investigate the causes that contribute to low retention levels, and provide some recommendation on how to raise retention levels to 90%.

⑦

To perform this research, we enlisted the aid of institutional research to run retention reports by discipline, gender, and ethnicity, and income. We created a survey to be distributed to composition and literature classrooms. This survey was designed ⑧ to expose any inherent weaknesses in classroom methodology, financial hardships, work schedules, language barriers, and disabilities. We also created a focus group of several English faculty to discuss real-time issues in the classroom that affect student retention.

⑨

After collecting all of the data, these are the contributing factors we found:

- lack of adequate financial aid
- students juggling work and school
- learning methodologies were not addressing students adequately
⑩ - the traditional 16-week term is not compatible with student completion goals
- the demand for online education is increasing due to its flexibility
- no technological innovation in classrooms

On the basis of these findings, *we conclude that decreases in student retention* ⑪ *are directly related to financial resources, incompatibility of long work hours and classroom hours, and teaching methodologies.* We further recommend that the Vice-President of Instruction appoint a task force of faculty and administrators to ⑫ formulate an appropriate response plan to address each of the contributing factors to low student retention.

⑬ — James Randolph, Ph.D.
Professor of English
Carlton College

⑭ — cc: Lucy Miller, Associate Dean of Communications

Figure: 8.5 Print Executive Summary Content Areas and Spacing Requirements

EXERCISES

1. Compose a persuasive internal proposal for solving a problem that stifles productivity on the job **OR** a problem in college that inhibits learning or safety. Choose a problem where the resolution depends on common sense, observation, and moderate research. The content areas below are the minimum required and **MANDATORY**
   - Introduction
   - Statement of the problem
   - Proposed solution
   - Proposed Plan
   - Costs
   - Benefits
   - Conclusion

© Rawpixel.com/Shutterstock.com

WORKING TO WIN!

STRATEGIES YOU SHOULD KNOW!

OVERVIEW

This section is dedicated to best practices in the workplace because the corporate environment is ever changing. Technology has a lot to do with this continually evolving world, but there are other factors as well. Take for instance, human behavior, group and individual priorities, levels of expectation, and perhaps one of the most important, how you and your colleagues perceive each other. Being aware of these things is the easy part. Being able to adjust and respond to them is the difficult part if you want to be successful.

And isn't success what it is all about? Yes, so how you respond to the ever-changing demands of your workplace will require a specific strategy for a specific occasion. This is where 'best practices' comes into play. It's impossible to be able to predict every single situation you may have to confront and respond to. You'll need a little help which is why this section has great value. Think of it as a quick reference guide with business writing tips, advice on office etiquette, and appropriate ways to interact with colleagues. And don't forget, the old may not be new and trendy. There are still some old-school office practices that have value and are sorely missed.

In short, this section will help you be able to function in a variety of situations that require strong writing skills, effective verbal communication, honesty, trustwBestorthiness, and thoughtfulness. It is presented in a series of brief, blog-like segments that are concise and reader friendly. Some subjects included are the importance of trustworthiness, being aware of your audience and how best to persuade them, the importance of networking, and making sure your documents are both accurate and the appropriate length.

BEST PRACTICE #1: THE THREE Cs OF TEAMWORK

© Pressmaster/Shutterstock.com

COMMUNICATION

What are the real benefits of teamwork in business? Why is teamwork increasingly important? Teamwork and team building are being used in business environments where the nature of the work is complex or multi-faceted, not to mention fast-paced. Working in isolation as a single contributor may not be as productive as several colleagues with different skills working toward a single goal. Successful teams rely on three effective mechanisms: **communication, collaboration, and coordination**. I will discuss each of these mechanisms over the course of three posts, the first being this one which is dedicated to 'communication'.

What is Effective Business Communication?

It is a successful exchange of ideas between colleagues or team members that produces solutions to problems, improvements in process, setting expectations, knowledge sharing, and creating awareness. In short, effective communication assures quality in products and services.

The Rules of Effective Business Communication

- It should be concise.
- It should present information in the form of a well thought out plan.
- It should be clear and easy to understand.
- It should speed up the decision-making process.
- It should be inherently persuasive. That is, the material or information being presented should be convincing and factual.

Forms of Business Communcation

- Correspondence
- Proposals
- Reports
- Meetings
- Informal Discussions
- Presentations

Verbal Interaction and the Team Meeting

Rules and forms of communication are obvious. What is not obvious is the manner in which team members or colleagues verbally interact with each other. Be aware that you are a member of a team, which means each person has a voice in the process. When making comments or presenting information, be sure to invite your colleagues to respond with questions, improvements or enhancements, possible redundancies, or even errors of which you may not be aware.

- **Consider Your Audience** Your audience is your team, colleagues, or stakeholders. Written and verbal communication must not be overly informal. Think of the tone in which you are communicating. When writing, do not fall into 'text talk' or 'sofa chat'. At the same time, do not be overly formal. Remember, you are not at a back yard barbeque, nor are you addressing Congress. This advice also applies to verbal communication. The most important skill is being able to identify your audience and adapt your tone and style of communication to the situation.

- **Question, Listen, and Encourage** When working within your team, think of yourself as a teacher or facilitator. Yes, you should invite questions and comments, but you should also take it one step further. The roles of teacher and facilitator focus on developing a healthy exchange between students and attendees. What is the best way to accomplish this? Question, listen, and encourage. Question your team members on their points of view. Make a concerted effort to listen and show sincere interest in their ideas. When comments or feedback display creativity or ingenuity, encourage more dialogue. Invite your colleagues to explore their ideas and report back to the group.

- **Stay on Point** Whether facilitating or communicating within a team meeting, stay on point. Follow the agenda. Be aware of time constraints even as you question, listen, and encourage. This burden does not always fall to the person who called the meeting. Each member has a responsibility to make valuable contributions.

Next time, look forward to my discussion of the second 'C', the benefits of collaboration in the team environment.

BEST PRACTICE #2: THE THREE Cs OF TEAMWORK

COLLABORATION

In the last blog post, I talked about teamwork in the workplace being more effective when communication, collaboration, and coordination are at the center. I began the discussion focusing on the importance of effective communication. It should be concise. It should present information in the form of a well thought out plan. It should be clear and easy to understand. It should speed up the decision making process. And it should be

© Konstantin Chagin/Shutterstock.com

inherently persuasive, which speaks directly to the level of collaboration a strong team must have to be successful. Without communication, there can be no real collaboration.

What is Collaboration?

Collaboration is a group process through which colleagues come together to craft solutions and improve processes not limited to one individual idea.

What Does it Mean to Collaborate?

Collaborating means:

- Everyone has a voice at the table
- Being perceived as a good partner
- Valuing different viewpoints
- Coming across as a common united front

Three Essentials in the Collaborative Process

- **Engage Your Partners** – Team members should share knowledge. Knowledge sharing is a healthy and productive means by which the group can arrive at the best solution.
- **Capture Ideas and Action Items** – Team members should keep an accurate record of meeting notes. Some alternative forms of note taking can include diagrams or flow charts that visually depict innovative proposals.

- **Recognize Ideas** – Team members should give credit where credit is due. A pat on the back, a nod at the table, and a simple "I agree" can go a long way. There is no stronger motivation than positive feedback.

Two Must-Have's to Make it Work

- **Build Relationships** – It is absolutely essential to build relationships among your team members. Take time to build personal relationships by getting to know each other. During this process, strengths, and opportunities can be discovered and used to the best advantage of the team.
- **Foster Trust** – Being able to depend on your colleagues to deliver tasks on time and in detail is also absolutely essential. Trust is the confidence. And confidence that each member will fully contribute to the group eliminates pressure and unnecessary stress.

The Big Advantages

© Vadim Georgiev/Shutterstock.com

Since collaboration is now a hot item in the workplace, the advantages are not hard to spot. Collaborative teams bring together **different viewpoints** because teams are frequently pulled from different talent pools or departments to achieve one goal. Because a variety of ideas will be put on the table, it's much easier to develop **ingenuity** when there is more than one option. Good ideas give way to better ideas. Groups who collaborate tend to be more inventive and resourceful. Collaboration can also bring a certain **unity** to the decision making process. Having more than one stakeholder ensures that team decisions will be reflective of all and not one, thus **eliminating perceived bias**. Lastly, a **quick delivery** of the product is likely to occur. Having several hands on deck is an automatic advantage when considering a collection of talent, skills, and intellect.

Next time, look forward to my discussion of the third 'C', the benefits of coordination in the team environment.

BEST PRACTICE #3: THE THREE Cs OF TEAMWORK

© Rawpixel.com/Shutterstock.com

COORDINATION

In the last blog, I talked about collaboration as part of an overall team structure that helps colleagues come together to craft solutions and improve processes. Communication is also a key component in collaboration, for without communication there can be no real collaboration. And without coordination, the fruits of communication and collaboration are lost.

The Three 'C' Model

COMMUNICATION * COLLABORATION * COORDINATION

What is **coordination**? It is the glue that holds the model together. Coordination within teams is simply ensuring the job gets done. If you find yourself in the role of 'team leader', you must ask yourself two questions. What is my role and what will it take to get the job done?

The Role of Team Coordinator

- The team leader or team coordinator serves as a primary liaison between team members.
- The team coordinator is responsible for making sure team members are keenly aware of their specific roles and function within the group.
- Team coordinators are also tasked with the authority to make critical decisions when the team cannot arrive at a consensus.

The Responsibilities of the Team Coordinator

Think of a team coordinator as a coach in a team sport. The team is made up of individuals each with particular skills or talents. The team coordinator must channel all of these talents into an effective force that will bring a project to completion.

The Team Coordinator Must:

- Have a long term vision of the work to be done
- Know each team member
- Define team roles
- Ensure the team has a common goal
- Make sure all team members know their assignments
- Leverage resources and specific skills of the team
- Create a workable plan
- Have the correct tools available for the team to complete their tasks
- Encourage effective communication among the team
- Conduct periodic checkpoints to determine progress against deliverables.

What Happens When Coordination is Absent?

A lack of coordination within a project team can decrease productivity, complicate processes, and delay the completion of projects. Below are some common signs:

- **Duplication of Work** – A usual sign of a lack of coordination within a project team is redundancy. Redundancy is caused by a lack of communication. With redundancy, an organization will spend double the efforts, materials, and time to produce the same item twice. Redundancy typically results from the poor coordination of a project team.
- **Lost Information** – Teams must effectively share information to function at an optimal level. When this information is not readily available as needed within the team, the lack of information can create a cascading effect that will damage the team. Lost information can lead to delays.
- **Delays on Deliverables** – Deliverables are the building blocks of an overall project. Deliverables can be reports, documents, and software upgrades; anything that contributes to the successful delivery of the project to the customer. One of the signs that team lacks coordination is called 'delay' and delays on deliverables can cause a project to miss a completion date.

© Peshkova/Shutterstock.com

The Big Advantages of Team Coordination

The advantages of team coordination are realistic. Roles, responsibilities and deadlines are assigned. Informal coaching and mentoring takes place, which benefits the group. It ensures a consolidation of work that can be measurable, attainable, and time constrained. It provides a single access point of communication between the team coordinator and business executives.

BEST PRACTICE #4: THE ABCs OF EMAIL

© camilla$$/Shutterstock.com

Even though email is one of the most important forms of electronic communication, it is one of the most frequently misunderstood in terms of its impact on public opinion, professional dealings, and even personal relationships. In short, email carries a punch particularly when you are communicating with your colleagues and supervisors on the job. It's powerful and it's effective.

So, how could something so entrenched in our everyday lives be misunderstood? It's easy to overlook flaws in things that are familiar just as you overlook the annoying habit of a brother who never removes his empty dish from the table after dinner.

Because of our familiarity with email, we fail to run through the ABCs, those basic things that need to be paid attention to, yet are frequently missed when performing what we think is a good 'proofread' before we click the 'send' button. Let's recite.

A is for Announcing Your Subject Effectively

Subject lines are very important if you want your message to be opened right away. It must be 'attention-getting' and it must be brief. While you may think of it as a simple thing to compose, it can actually be quite difficult. Think of it as a three to five word banner that clearly tells the recipient what your message is about. Those few words can communicate urgency, a call to action, or delivery of important information.

B is for Being Aware of Your Tone

Because you are engaging in a business dialogue, you must always remember to keep your tone business-like, unbiased, and emotion free. It's easy to forget to do this because you probably spend more time in personal email and texting, which is a highly informal environment. You should not use slang or colloquialisms, and should avoid contractions. For example, forget about OMG, LOL, 'see what I'm saying', 'hooked up', and 'I got this'. Do not substitute 'u' for you, 'ur for your, or 'r' for are. This type of informal communication is not appropriate in a business environment.

C is for Checking Your Word Count

The length of your message is extremely important. Typically, an email should be no longer than 250 words. Your message may be informational, responding to an on-going issue, or arguing a change of course in procedure. Regardless, you need to focus on being concise. If the subject requires more than 250 words, think about attaching relevant documents that provide additional detail. Remember, your recipients 'inbox' is almost always full. Do yourself and your colleagues a favor and avoid long-winded messages.

D is for Doing Away With Misspelled Words

One of the most glaring, memorable mistakes you can make is failing to proofread your message for misspelled words. Always perform a manual spell check. Don't rely on auto spell check to catch your errors because your email settings may not be set up to perform this. Mistakenly, you will believe all is okay when in reality all is not. Another 'trap' in auto spell check is the proposed substitution. The proposed word may be spelled correctly, but not the right word to stress your meaning. For instance, if you type the word 'principle' to denote value, spell check could incorrectly read it as a misspelled word and offer to make the change. The change it might suggest is 'principal'. If you allow the change without manually proofreading, you have made a word usage error which might as well be a misspelled word.

E is for Eliminating Grammatical Errors

Manually proofread your messages for misspelled words. Do no rely on automatic spell check. Do not rely on automatic grammar checks. If you're unsure about your skill in tracking down grammar errors, here's a good technique. It's simple. Read your message out loud. If a sentence doesn't feel right as you're reading along, stop and reread the problematic passage out loud again. Then look for the grammar mistake. It will be the there. It could be incorrect sentence structure, a missing word, or a case in which your subject and verb do not agree. You can also catch long wordy sentences [run-on], or a sentence that lacks a subject or verb causing it to be an incomplete sentence [fragment]. Bottom line, nothing is a good substitute for using your own brain.

BEST PRACTICE #5: PERSUASION AND OCCASION IN INTERNAL PROPOSALS

© Gustavo Frazao/Shutterstock.com

You are a professional. You want to be successful. You want your good ideas to be noticed and implemented. What's the magic formula? You write to persuade. You create carefully crafted internal proposals that will cause your supervisor to accept your recommendations. That's easily said. The hard part is knowing the difference between a document that persuades a supervisor to accept a solution to an old problem, and a document that tells the story of an old problem.

One of the 'booby traps' in business writing that can cause your ideas to go unnoticed is telling a story rather than providing a solution. This is called 'writing about the occasion'. For example, my students have, in more than one instance, attempted to write a persuasive proposal, but instead penned a narrative that told the story of a problem rather than presenting a solution. There is a big difference between occasion and persuasion; one of which you should be fully aware.

What is 'Writing About the Occasion'?

- Writing about the occasion leaves out relevant valuable detail.
- Writing about the occasion gives too much time to tangentially related personal experience and the opinions/reactions of colleagues.
- Writing about the occasion is background that overspends itself in immaterial details of what has taken place.
- Writing about the occasion does not lay out a clear recommendation and solution.

✗ Don't Write About the Occasion

You have discovered a way to increase productivity in the workplace. You want to submit an informal internal proposal to your supervisor. These are the things you think you must cover in your proposal:

- You feel you must describe what's going on.
- You think you need to list all who are involved.
- You are determined to include the opinions of your colleagues.
- You are convinced you must include your big ideas and thoughts because you're the one who has the solution.
- You'll write it all down from beginning to end in a long string of paragraphs.

This is exactly what you do. Congratulations! You have just written about the occasion of 'poor productivity' in the workplace. It might make an interesting tale, but remember your supervisor doesn't expect short-short stories from you. They expect 'usable' ideas that give way to solid solutions.

Write About the Solution

So how do you compose a document that recommends, proposes a plan, and provides a solution without telling a story? You follow a blueprint. A blueprint is something as simple as a list of content sub-headings. If you keep to specific content and clear sub-headings, you'll be safe. Think of these areas as a table of contents, or even an outline. Below is a list of solution driven content headings in internal proposals:

- Subject Line
- Background
- Statement of the Problem
- Proposed Solution
- Proposed Plan
- Costs
- Benefits

Confining your proposal to specific areas of discussion will keep you away from relating a story. It will leave you little room to digress and keep you to the job at hand. Structure, focus, clarity, and detail are essential. We all have a tendency to want to jump out there and start talking about what needs to be done, but this is not what needs to happen when it comes to writing a proposal. Stick with content areas that are organized under short, clear sub-headings to avoid becoming a writer of short stories.

 Can Occasion and Persuasion Cohabitate?

It is possible for the two to happily occupy the same document on a very limited basis in the following areas:

- The **background** in the proposal would be an appropriate place to include some personal on the job experience if it serves as an 'attention getting' device, or an anecdote that helps bring the problem into greater focus.
- The **statement of the problem** is also another possible place to include a little story telling. Sometimes relating a 'real experience' is necessary to help convince and elicit an emotional response in the reader. This technique is called 'pathos' in argument theory. It is the use of language or stories that emotionally bind an audience to a

subject and is likely to persuade an audience to change position. In the case of an internal proposal being submitted to your supervisor arguing an increase in safety protocols, a very limited description of on the job accidents could prove helpful.

BEST PRACTICE #6: PICK UP THE TELEPHONE!

© BlueSkyImage/Shutterstock.com

Effective written communication is absolutely essential in the workplace. I emphasize its importance in my book. I stress we must be strategic and persuasive when it comes to implementing beneficial change. As much as I believe in the concept of creating a smart, intelligent image of yourself through your writing, it's not the only means.

Pick up the telephone.

Yes, we live in a data age of electronic words that have pretty much replaced the traditional, "Hi, how are you...and... I have a quick question that will take care of the entire issue." The obvious concern with the present state of things is the lack of human-to-human 'real voice' communication. The exchange of ideas in our current environment rests on three main platforms: instant messaging, email, and texting. We've grown used to it. We love it. Somehow we have lulled ourselves into the complacency of avoiding a real conversation because we think it takes more time. But perhaps, it's time to rethink this digital substitution and think 'old school' instead. There are many advantages to picking up the telephone.

© Attl Tibor/Shutterstock.com

- **No Mistakes in Tone** - The first is safeguarding your tone and avoiding mistakes of intention. Quite simply, you avoid SENDING THE WRONG MESSAGE. In section two of my book, I stress the importance of tone. It's easy to inadvertently deposit your emotional state in an email, text, or instant message which, in turn, can cause unintended consequences. By picking up the telephone, you eliminate the guesswork. The tone and inflection of your voice, the conversational back and forth, the impromptu humor, and discussion leaves no room for error.
- **Relationship Building** – Building strong working relationships with your colleagues is very important and can likely contribute to your ultimate success. You may have heard the quote by John Donne, "No man is an island entire of itself. Everyman is a piece of the continent, a part of the main...". This is exactly right in the business world. Teamwork is everything. And you can't foster teamwork without building relationships. You can't build 'real' relationships with only email and instant messaging. There must be some human contact to give those digital words life.
- **Cutting Down the Email Chain** – Texting is great for brief questions and confirmations, but not for conversations. When the text messages get too long and begin to go on for what seems like forever, you know when it's time to stop and dial the number. The same is true with email. These types of messages should be brief,

and should not go on forever. To avoid these never ending chains, pick up the phone. One five-minute conversation could be equal to fourteen emails.

- **Immediate Response** – Writing takes time. Time is precious during the workday. Why wait for a reply to an email, when you can get your answer much faster? Remember, everyone's inbox is full. When you send an email, you get prioritized. Don't get prioritized. Get your answer quickly.

BEST PRACTICE #7: WOMEN AND INTERNAL NETWORKING

© michaeljung/Shutterstock.com

In previous posts, I have always stressed the fundamentals of persuasive business writing found in my book, *The Guide to Persuasive Business Writing: A New Model that Gets Results*. But lately, an important book, *Lean In* by Sheryl Sandberg has come to my attention. It's an honest, frank work that focuses on an untapped talent pool in the business world. It continues offering vital information on how these talented individuals can become leaders, champions, and partners.

Who are the people that make up this untapped resource?

Women.

At first sight, you might think this is just another self-help book full of advice you've already heard. I did, until I spoke with a female executive in a Fortune 500 corporation. I suddenly realized a simple truth. Chances are many women in the business world have lived the challenges presented

© Anton Gvozdikov/Shutterstock.com

in Sheryl Sandberg's book and may not have realized that there are reasonable and available options for overcoming these challenges.

What does all of this come down to? It comes down to women being assertive and understanding the value of internal networking. It comes down to collaboration and communication. There are companies that encourage women to seek a more visible role as senior leaders.

In my conversation with an executive who is currently involved in a women's internal networking group, I asked, what is the biggest value? She responded, "It's the opportunity to meet with my peers, other women, and be sponsored by senior leaders who are also women." She went on to explain how rewarding it was to be in a group with like-minded high performing women with ambition. But most importantly, she stressed the importance of having 'confidants', other women who share the same goals and challenges.

I pressed for more specific reasons on how women could benefit from internal networking circles. She said, "...it gives you the opportunity to meet peers from other areas of the company and expand your awareness of opportunities within the organization."

As I understand it, there are three big advantages to networking circles:

- You build relationships.
- You are able to increase awareness of greater leadership opportunities.
- You build knowledge with specific discussions on issues that help women to increase their effectiveness and exposure in the workplace.

© Billion Photos/Shutterstock.com

Being a teacher, I needed more examples of real-time value, so I asked her what chapters in the book have 'stayed' with you, that is, the biggest simplest rules to remember? Quickly, she said chapters two and four.

Chapter two according to Sandberg is time to "Sit at the Table." So what does this chapter boil down too I asked? She said, "...from what I have learned from reading the book is that women should take their proper place and not defer to eat the children's table, be assertive."

She went on to talk about chapter four, "It's a Jungle Gym, not a Ladder." I asked her to elaborate and she spoke about yet another great metaphor, the jungle gym. Apparently, the author wants women to understand that the way to success is not always a straight line. Lateral moves are good, but sometimes backwards moves can be made to build your skill set and advance.

So, if someone were to ask me what was the value in sitting down and talking to someone actively involved in a women's group whose intent is to expand their reach professionally and personally, I would have to say this: Think Chess.

© LIUDMILA ERMOLENKO/
Shutterstock.com

It's all about strategy and patience. Be strategic and recognize that women represent the great untapped pool of talent. Be strategic and do something about organizing this vast pool. Be patient and know that knowledge building and forging relationships may take time, but the rewards can be great.

In his review of *Lean In*, by Sheryl Sandberg, Sir Richard Branson, chairman of the Virgin Group stated, "…women in leadership roles is good for business as well as society."

BEST PRACTICE #8: SURVIVING ETHICAL SKIRMISHES IN THE WORKPLACE

Persuasive Business Writing involves more than giving your great ideas:

- Currency [value]
- Articulation [voice]
- Selling Power [promotion]
- Endurance [strength]

It involves giving your great ideas an honest and principled foundation based more on the good of all rather than the good of one. In the hit HBO series, *A Game of Thrones*, several warring noble houses repeatedly clash in their quest for the "Iron Throne." They resort to the most questionable tactics to seize this great prize as their own. It is obvious that ethics and ethical behavior do not factor into their strategies. From that world to the business world in which you will likely find yourself, the great prize could be a corner office with a view, a dedicated administrative assistant, a six figure income, and an annual bonus with stock options.

© Tashatuvango/Shutterstock.com

Unlike the nobles in *A Game of Thrones*, you must stay within the ethical boundaries of 'Corporate America'. And staying within these boundaries means understanding the nature of ethical behavior. It doesn't always boil down to the simple difference between 'right and wrong'. More often than not, you may find yourself in an ethical skirmish where the right thing to do may not be fitting, the wrong thing to do is not an option, and the in-between still leaves you with an un-easy feeling.

Surviving an ethical skirmish in the workplace requires a strong sense of self. What does this mean exactly? It's simple. It's when you realize it's not about you all of the time. So forget the notion that a skirmish has to involve another party. The most challenging ethical skirmishes may be a conflict between 'you' and 'you' when trying to answer questions such as:

- Is sharing a good thing?
- Is taking responsibility a good thing?
- How much commitment should I show?
- Am I being truthful and honest?

What do these questions of ethical behavior have to do with persuasive business writing? It has the obvious. You must be able to communicate your ability to solve problems and improve processes in a fair and principled manner. And to do this, you must be able to survive ethical skirmishes in the workplace.

Two Big Rules of Survival

© Aquir/Shutterstock.com

Rule #1–Avoid the 'Me-Condition' Try not to base all of your ideas, choices, and decisions on personal interest. Self-interest can be a good thing, but it can also run contrary to other people's best interest.

Rule #2–Test Your Conclusions When situation and circumstance come into play, it can be hard to avoid the 'me-condition' and come to the most ethical conclusion. So ask yourself three simple questions:

- How might this conclusion benefit me?
- How might this benefit hurt or help other people?
- In the long run, how might this conclusion contribute to the kind of person I ultimately want to be?

Remember, more often than not, you may find yourself in an ethical skirmish in which your character could be tried. And as I state in my book, it's hard not to think of your own best interest first. Because of this, you should practice the rules of survival being fully aware you may be engaged in a clash of conscious in what I refer to as the 'grey zone', a place where interpreting the difference between right and wrong behavior can be tested.

BEST PRACTICE #9: WRITE A WINNING PROPOSAL

What Type of Proposal Should You Expect to Write?

Generally, large companies or corporations have entire departments staffed with professional proposal writers to write formal proposals. You should expect to write an informal internal proposal.

What is it Exactly?

What's a proposal? They come in various shapes and sizes. They can be either solicited or unsolicited. They can be as short as an email and as long as a ten page document. They are always persuasive in nature. In short, proposals are arguments.

Internal Proposal – The **purpose** of an internal proposal will be to persuade your boss or supervisor to:

- Change a process
- Solve a problem
- Purchase products, services, or pursue activities
- Conduct research or make changes in policies

© Leungchopan/Shutterstock.com

The **message** will always be persuasive, fact based, and verifiable. The **benefit** can come in the form of improvements in productivity and profitability and will likely contribute to another accomplishment line on your resume.

- *The Unsolicited Internal Proposal* – These are proposals that have not been requested by a manager. These types of proposals are opportunities to cast you as a proactive, forward-thinking employee. This is your time to boost your image. For example, suppose you realize that the office network's current operations system slows down the production of sales orders. Changing operating systems would increase productivity. You write a memo describing what is going on, what you want to do, why you want to do it, what it will cost, and what will be the overall benefit. This an unsolicited internal proposal is a means to sell your creative ideas.
- *A Solicited Internal Proposal* – These are proposals are requested by a manager or supervisor. There may not be a need for you come up with 'the answer' or solve the problem. Your boss may have already provided the solution and simply requests you measure its viability. This is still an opportunity for you to gain some good exposure because you will have to use your critical thinking skills and make a recommendation.

WRITING A PROPOSAL FOR WORK

© Gustavo Frazao/Shutterstock.com

What Not to Expect

First, do not expect to write formal proposals unless you have been hired specifically to serve on a proposal team. These proposals are comprehensive, well-researched documents that can be ten or more pages. Corporations have entire departments staffed with professional proposal writers to create these.

What to Expect

The type of proposal you more than likely find yourself writing will be *an internal unsolicited proposal discussed earlier.* It will be in the form of a medium length email or a memo. Remember, this informal proposal does not have to be written on the level of a formal proposal written by professional proposal writer. It should not exceed more than two pages if presented as a memo, and no more than a six paragraph email.

Expect it to be Persuasive

It will need to convince your manager or supervisor that your ideas will work. In a nutshell, the benefits produced will far outweigh the costs of implementation. Your manager will need to believe that:

- You fully understand the organization's mission: productive, profitable, and innovative
- You fully understand the organization's operations
- You fully understand the necessity of the proposal
- You know the solution
- You know how to implement the solution

BEST PRACTICE #10: WRITING AND THE MANAGEMENT OF EXPECTATIONS

© Jirsak/Shutterstock.com

It would be a wonderful thing to know exactly what people expect of you over and above your duties and responsibilities on the job. You'd know exactly what to do to meet these additional expectations in your day to day performance. Being that the probabilities are high that most of the population cannot read minds, you must devise other ways to manage the expectations of your audience, namely, your colleagues, managers, or key stakeholders. *Consider your audience.*

Who is my Audience?

You already know your audience will either be your colleagues, managers, or key stakeholders. Now, you must learn to write *TO* their beliefs, needs, and expectations in a way that will '*win the day*'. That is, the means by which you can accomplish the goals laid out in your report, proposal, or executive summary.

Your Goal Should Be a Simple One: SUCCESS

- The acceptance of your proposed solution to a problem
- The acceptance of your proposed improvement to a process
- The acceptance of the progress you have made in a key on-going project.

How Can I Know Their Expectations?

- Be aware of the project's or division's success objectives. These are specific things that must be achieved to demonstrate success in your department.
- Be diligent on the job. Keep your ears open, stay informed, and engaged in the workplace.

Here's How Managing Expectations Works

© Brasil Creativo/Shutterstock.com

If you want to convince your manager to give you a shorter work week for the same pay, you'll need to understand why he/she wouldn't want to give you a shorter work week even though you'll be working the same hours. In other words, you must figure out what she believes on the subject of shorter work weeks. This is where you begin to make assumptions or guesses about her feelings on the subject of shorter work weeks. When you begin to make these assumptions or educated guesses, you begin to write to the needs of your audience.

You are a pharmaceuticals warehouse supervisor. Keeping track of inventory is an obvious priority. You know that inventory levels have been inaccurate in the last two accounting periods. You want to propose a solution to the problem, but before you present a 'proposed plan', you must try to figure out the expectations of your manager with regard to this problem. In short, you present your plan in such a way as to address what **YOU THINK** his *beliefs and expectations* may be given the current shrinkage problem. When you begin to make a mental list, it may look something look this if you were to write it down.

Walk a Mile in Another Pair of Shoes

The Director of Corporate Logistics distributes a monthly newsletter that highlights shrinkage and how it decreases company profits. You know your manager keeps a close eye on this issue and measures warehouse shrinkage monthly, then reports this to corporate logistics. You also know that your manager constantly talks about adding more technology and wants to be noticed by the Director of Logistics. You also know that your facility manager would like to avoid hiring more security personnel.

Then Present Your Solution

This will be the first paragraph in your proposal

Based on last month's warehouse inventory, there has been an eight per cent increase in shrinkage. Our monthly sales figures do not support this high level of 'missing' merchandise. Nor can we afford to hire more security guards. Therefore, I would like to recommend a technological upgrade in our present security system. It will help us accomplish our goals without increasing payroll.

© Oilyy/Shutterstock.com

Figure it Out

When you have a strong idea of what may be going on in the mind of your audience, you will have a strong idea of how to sell your idea.

This is the same as building a strong persuasive document. *A persuasive document is an <u>argument</u>.* And building a good argument starts with creating the foundation upon which it rests. This foundation is *the need to know your audience* which brings us back to the three key considerations in effective written business communication.

BEST PRACTICE #11: WRITING AND LENGTH, HOW MUCH IS TOO MUCH?

© Elena Elisseeva/Shutterstock.com

One of the greatest realizations seasoned professionals come to find out is the fact that 'you don't know what you don't know', meaning, you may not realize that even though you have years of experience in the office, this does not necessarily mean you are a great business writer.

Business writing is an art and a skill. It is artistic because a well-put-together business document can be a beautiful thing when it accomplishes your purpose. It is a skill because it takes practice and the knowledge.

One key consideration is *LENGTH.*

CONSIDER THE LENGTH of your document. This is very important because a reader can easily become distracted, disengaged, or outright bored if there seems to be no end in sight. What is an acceptable length? It depends on the document. Email, interoffice memos, letters, reports, and internal proposals have different objectives. The objective drives the length, that is, the reason why you are writing the document. But it doesn't just stop at its reason for being.

You Must Also Take Into Consideration:

- **The Recipient** – Have some knowledge of the individual to whom you are writing. Is this person a stickler for detail? Or does this person prefer 'broad brush strokes' rather than getting bogged down in the minutiae?
- **The Subject** – Some subjects require more length than others. Longer topics should be summarized in an executive summary and detail can be provided in an attachment or appendix, satisfying the person who wants details, but not overwhelming those that want broad brush strokes. Always remember, *LENGTH IS CONTINGENT ON THE TYPE OF DOCUMENT.*
- **The Type of Document** – Different types of documents have varying lengths. Below, are a few examples.

 ## Types of Documents and Their Lengths

- **Email** – [200 – 250 words] Email is considered a 'brief' form of communication. Be concise. Emails should be no more than three paragraphs. There are basically two types: informational and promotional. Informational email are exactly that — a means of imparting information. They can also be persuasive, meaning they are small arguments that are meant to sway opinion. Persuasive email tends to be longer than informational because you must be careful to include such persuasive elements such as a claim, support, and considerations of audience. Informational email should absolutely be no longer than 200 words.
- **Interoffice Memos** – [300 – 350 words] it can be hard to tell the difference between the traditional memo and an email message. Memos frequently do not have the 'MEMORANDUM' banner at the top anymore. They are frequently sent in the form of an email or as an email attachment. So, is it email or what? No, memos are not email. They are longer. They can use various techniques to layout information such as bullets, sub-headings, and the occasional table if it is very small. In short, memos include much more detailed information. They are a more formal document.
- **Letters** – [250 – 300 words] Letters have an inherent amount of power that sets them apart from email and memos, but they must not exceed one page. They may be composed to gather information

or show appreciation. They can solicit new business or convey bad news. They can announce promotions or terminate employment.

- **Reports** – [up to 500 words] Reports have the luxury of added length. There are several types of reports: progress, term projects, activity, and feasibility to name a few. The length can vary depending on the type. Five hundred words would more than likely be a business progress report. Feasibility reports would be appropriate at this length. Activity reports can top out at 300 words depending on the activity.

- **Internal Proposals** – [500 – 600 words] Proposals come in various shapes and sizes. They can be either internal or external. They can be either solicited or unsolicited. They can be as short as an email and as long as a ten-page document. They have the luxury of being longest document you might every write. They are always persuasive in nature. In short, proposals are arguments, which require length to be truly effective.

© garagestock/Shutterstock.com

What is important to note when it comes to length of business documents is to keep the meaning of the word *concise* firmly rooted in your mind. When you are in the workplace, you are not in a classroom. You are not writing research papers, essays, responses, or summaries. You are crafting a message that your reader must realize quickly and clearly.

BEST PRACTICE #12: SELECTING QUALITY DATA

If you asked a room packed full with one hundred college level sopho-mores, "What is the value of detail?", what do you think would be the response? But let's make this more interesting. Ask those same college sophomores what the value of detail is if their political science final exam will consist of only three essay questions. Chances are you would get a highly respectable response to the value of detail. No doubt you would more than likely hear shouts of words, words, and more words.

If you asked a room packed full with one hundred investment bankers the same question, what do you think would be the response? Again, let's drill down to specifics. Ask those same investment bankers what the value of detail is when a three billion dollar merger is resting on a conversion of stock plan. No doubt, you would surely hear shouts of numbers, numbers, and more numbers.

Words and numbers, numbers and words, it doesn't take rocket sci-ence to figure out that 'when *a big lot of something*' is riding on a single document leading with all the support you can muster is the best way to go to meet your goal. But, remember the last post? It was all about length, correct? It explained the importance of decision making when considering length. Now, consider the importance of judging the quality and magnitude of detail.

 ## THE DEVIL'S IN THE DETAILS FOR BETTER OR WORSE

Just as length of a document is an important consideration, the same goes for detail. Let's simplify and call it data or support. Regardless which word catches your attention, both mean the same. The bottom line, data and support can work for or against you. Too much, too little, too weak, too irrelevant, too ambiguous, it all matters. So, pay close attention to the '*kind*' of detail.

 ## HOW DO I JUDGE WHAT IS THE BEST?

Giving attention to these areas with which to judge your data will help you select the most effectual means to sell your solution to the problem or your idea for a better process.

- Think Quality
- Think Usefulness
- Think Relevance

 ## THE ART OF DETAIL AND HOW TO PRESENT IT

Figuring out how to present your data in the most compressive, concise, and readable way is an art.

The How To's

- **Light on Text, Heavy on Visualization** – Text is okay, but try to use PowerPoint Slides, Tables, and Charts as much as you can. Too many words will lose your reader even if there are numbers embedded. **This is where '*quality*' comes into play.** Pick the best presentation mode so as not to distract your audience. Keep it simple and clear. It is important to interpret what the numbers are saying, '*sales are up 12% because...*' Communicate this with the 'least' populated visual that will get your point across.
- **Merge Your Data** – You must always strive to be concise. Yes, detail matters, but you must be the judge of how much is too much.

As the case with length, how long is too long? My best advice is to narrow to the most essential for making your case. **This is where 'relevance' comes into play.** For instance, *'call volume is down 6% due to the month being two business days shorter than the prior month'*. Gather all your data and judge it according to the most relevant, then eliminate the rest.

- **Scrutinize for Accuracy** – Researching and gathering data is no simple task depending on your project or goal. It is easy to accumulate and accumulate. But as I said earlier, it must be relevant. Not only must your data be relevant, it must be correct. **This is where** *'usefulness'* **comes into play.** Seek to find the most reputable sources or experts in the field to make your case. If your office setting is somewhat unique and you wish to make a more local case for change with local support, test it as a scientist would. Opinions and general story telling of what transpires during the day in a certain situation is not strong. Be ready to observe, measure, and take detailed notes that can be translated into hard statistics.

BEST PRACTICE #13: DELIVERING WHAT YOU PROMISE

© Brasil Creativo/Shutterstock.com

Delivering what you promise is crucial in the workplace. It not only reinforces your success, it also bolsters your trustworthiness. It is important to understand that delivering what you promise is a concept that applies to employee and employer. So, it is not enough to understand what *you* need to do to keep your promises. You must also understand what your employer needs to do to keep their promises. Making good on commitments is a golden rule. Not making good can create adverse effects for the employee, the employer, and business clients as well. Altogether, the overall well-being of your company can be threatened. So, let's take a brief look at how you can keep your promises, and how employers should keep their promises to you.

How Employees Can Keep Their Promises

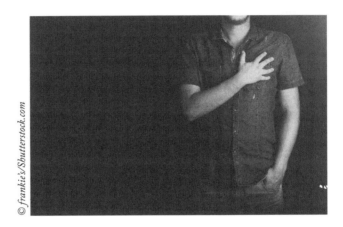

© frankie's/Shutterstock.com

It seems as if there is more pressure on an employee to deliver than an employer. It's certainly plausible given who has the most power. Clearly, the employer appears to have the most power because an employee doesn't want to be fired for poor performance. So, the pressure is indeed on an employee. Hanging on to a paycheck and benefits is major motivation when it comes to committing to things that may not be possible.

- **Don't Promise Unrealistic Delivery Dates** – Realize your constraints. Present realistic deadline dates for yourself and your team. Yes, being an independent contributor is great because you feel you are the master of your own destiny and are not dependent on others. But what if you are a member of a team? You cannot always predict who will complete tasks according to the schedule. You cannot always predict when you can complete tasks given 'life circumstances' that may pop up.

- **Be Realistic When It Comes to the Burdens of Workload** – Sometimes job responsibilities change and workload increases. And as I said earlier, employers sometimes underplay the real demands of a job. In either case, most people feel they can keep up regardless. Be thoughtful and above all, be honest with yourself and your manager. Do not commit to fully satisfying the demands of a position if it is not possible. Voice your concerns so that you can avoid being perceived as over promising and under delivering.

HOW EMPLOYERS CAN KEEP THEIR PROMISES

Most of us like to believe our employer will always follow through on assurances he or she has committed too. But sometimes this is not always the case. So, it is important to be aware of fundamental promises between employer and employee.

- **Employers should never be biased when granting promotions** – This is absolutely not supposed to occur. It compromises not only ethical principles, but practically speaking, customary human resource directives. And violating these directives can put the company at risk for civil suits given equal protection.
- **Employers should always be truthful about job responsibilities** – Remember the old saying, 'necessity is the mother of invention'? In some cases, if the pressure to fill a position is too great, necessity could entice an employer to stretch the truth when it comes to the realities of workload in a particular position.

- **Employers should never allow special privileges to a few** – Seniority and long-time friendships should not influence favors and privileges in a non-union environment. Still, this can occur. An employer or manager given the right circumstances may over promise that he or she will not be partial to specific employees, but may not keep that promise.

Ways to Avoid Overpromising:

- **Be honest with yourself** before making a commitment on delivery dates with your client or workload responsibilities with your employer. Can it be done?
- **Set realistic expectations** with your client and employer.
- **Communicate quickly and honestly.** If you can see that you are not living up to promises or delivery dates, do not wait until recovery is not possible. As soon as you see the 'danger signs' either in your general workload, scheduled date to roll out a product or solution, SPEAK UP.
- **Take ownership** if you fail to meet expectations. If you are part of a team, do not place the blame on other members. This is counterproductive and will cast a negative light on you.

© ImageFlow/Shutterstock.com

BEST PRACTICE #14: THE IMPORTANCE OF TRUST IN THE WORKPLACE

© Olivier Le Moal/Shutterstock.com

Remember when you were a kid? It was pretty clear what was good and what was bad. When you were good, there was ice cream in your future. When you were bad, it was off to the time out corner. It was never a case of either/or. Nowadays you're all grown up. You've figured out that the rules can be bent at times for one reason or the other. And sometimes you've probably indulged in rule bending because it was pretty harmless. Afterward, you may have felt a little uneasy about it, but you tell yourself, no laws were broken. No harm no foul, right? These are the questions that create a feeling of uneasiness when you're not sure you've made the right decision. It's important to know because it's a matter of 'trust'. Losing 'trust' in the workplace is a 'losing proposition'. Don't go there.

Being trustworthy is the rock solid foundation of who you are in the present and how you will be perceived in the future.

What Does it Mean to be Trustworthy?

There are certain things that shouldn't be done in the workplace. Things like plagiarizing, hiding information, exaggerating claims, copyright infringement, crossing cultural boundaries, and conflicts of interest.

Avoiding this type of behavior is part of what it means to be an honest, upright employee.

Being trustworthy means you live by a set of principles that govern ethical human behavior. These principles can come down to beliefs such as treating others as you would want to be treated. These principles can also come down to intuition, some inner feeling or moral compass that helps you decide what is right and what is wrong. It comes down to: Am I trustworthy? Or simply, what is the right thing to do?

A sense of justice, individual rights, and understanding the consequences of your actions have much to do with your sense of right and wrong. And your sense of right and wrong will guide your choices in the workplace and will project the degree of your trustworthiness among your colleagues.

© ONEVECTOR/Shutterstock.com

Don't be a Weasel

Weasels are by definition cunning and devious. You may find yourself in a location where situation and circumstance may affect how you understand the difference between right behavior and wrong behavior. This is the 'grey zone', a place in which a person has the opportunity to circumvent definitions of right and wrong behavior. In other words, the meanings could change due to extenuating circumstances. You may find yourself thinking of ways to '*go around*' or to '*avoid*'. Try not to find yourself in this position. It may feel like artful maneuvering when in fact you may be bending the rules to suit your own needs rather than those of your coworkers.

Some Guidelines to Avoid 'Weaseling-Out'

- Don't evade responsibility. Do not back out of commitments. Cultivate cooperative behavior that benefits the group.
- Don't be sneaky in your dealings, or try to achieve success by underhanded methods.

- Don't be cunning in order to advance selfish interests or hurt others.
- Don't be evasive in your communication with others. Be straightforward.
- Don't be intentionally vague or ambiguous in your conduct.
- Don't be deceptive in your actions, or mislead deliberately.
- Don't be cowardly. Display confidence. Try to set a good example when dealing with tough issues.

BEST PRACTICE #15: KEEPING THE 'MOOD' OUT OF THE MESSAGE

© Mialima/Shutterstock.com

Here's the thing about electronic communication in the business world nowadays. You rarely have to face the person on the other end so it becomes easy to hide behind a wall of transactions like 'reply and delete', 'follow-up, clean up, and forward'. In the section on 'tone' in my handbook, I wrote, "Do not think of email as some protective covering." Actually, it should go something like this, do not think of business writing as protective covering. It's anything but…..your writing and the tone you create in your messages can make you an open book, that is, open to other people's interpretation. Try not to let this happen.

You will send many messages in the workplace. Typically, most of them will be in the form of email and instant messaging. But depending on your job, you may also be tasked with more formal writing such as letters, memos, and progress reports to name a few.

Just as the singing contestants in the NBC series, *The Voice*, work to create the most beautiful tone and win the contest, you must also work to create the most appropriate tone in your business writing. How? By understanding the origin of tone and understanding what it takes to ensure your tone is always appropriate. Because the concept of tone is challenging and requires explanation and exercises, let's confine our discussion to two basic questions and some solid advice.

© Jezper/Shutterstock.com

Obvious Questions

What is tone?

- It's simple. 'Tone is Attitude'. And attitude is a state of mind that can be passed on in our words.

How do you know when your tone is appropriate?

- Your tone is appropriate when you take the 'mood out of the message'.

Expert Advice

© Tashatuvango/Shutterstock.com

Understand Emotional Mine Fields To keep the mood out of the message, know how to navigate the emotional mine fields. It's good to have a happy and upbeat attitude. But what about the times when you are not particularly happy and upbeat? These are the times when you must work to keep your mood out of your message. Think about sleepless nights, car troubles, family matters, and workload deadlines. These can drive the tone of your message and can wreak havoc in business communication. On the flip side, think about successes? Don't let them go to your head. Remember, you are a member of the team and must treat your colleagues with respect. It can be easy to slip into the, "I'm the king of the world" attitude (*Titanic*, Twentieth Century Fox, 1997).

Avoid Booby Traps in the Mine Fields As you make your way through the mine fields, don't be caught off guard and let your emotions lead you into the trap of.......

- **Being Contentious** – Don't use combative, bombastic language that suggests you are the conqueror and your colleagues are the conquered. Remember, cultivating teamwork means success for all.
- **Being Arrogant** – Don't use high flying, over-bloated language that would suggest you're the smartest in the room. Remember, it's possible you have a lot to learn from your teammates.
- **Being Bossy** – Don't use pretentious and domineering language as if you have been given the 'alpha' role. Remember, this decision likely rests with others.

Why is it Important to Keep the Mood Out of the Message?

© morenina/Shutterstock.com

- **Know that your mood can be caused by a single emotional response** or a conglomerate of them. Emotional responses include such things as anger, sadness, indifference, arrogance, and sarcasm. If you need to take some time, take the time and write when you are feeling calm, clear, and objective.
- **Know that your readers may misunderstand** and think your emotional response is their fault, or that you are directing your anger at them when in fact you are angry with yourself.
- **Know that electronic messages are practically eternal** in cyberspace. They may never be fully deleted either on the server or in the minds of your colleagues.
- **Know that words have consequences. What you think is acceptable or funny may be offensive to others. Do not use slang or overly familiar language. Do not use text-speak. Do not use expletives of any kind. Use Standard English and practice good grammar and spelling. Stay away from humor.**

The Golden Rule: the Message Creates the Image

© Ionut Catalin Parvu/Shutterstock.com

Some of your colleagues will never have the privilege of meeting you face to face and building a traditional working relationship. They will have to rely on your messaging. So, make your messaging worthy of 'who you truly are' and 'how you wish to be known'.

BEST PRACTICE #16: HANDWRITING IN THE AGE OF ELECTRONIC COMMUNICATION

© TaLaNoVa/Shutterstock.com

As an author and teacher in today's digital world, I am bombarded with email heralding messages of all sorts. But the messages that stand out most in my mind are the ones that arrived in a small envelope either slipped under my door or dropped in my mailbox.

One in particular was from a student thanking me for teaching a great class and letting me know how much she appreciated the effort. It would have been easy to send an email that would have been added to an already long list in my exploding inbox. Instead she chose to write a note that did not go unnoticed. Here was an individual who chose to express a sentiment in a genuinely real way.

In this age of electronic communication, it is easy to overlook the simple value of a handwritten note. Why bother when you can email, text, or send digital greeting cards? It's easier to tweet, post, email, or pin. Its fast, it's cheap, and unremarkable. But isn't it better to do something thoughtful and unexpected that differentiates your message from others?

Where is the inherent value in handwritten notes? It's authenticity. It's not just the words you put to paper, but the deeper message you send. Ask yourself, when was the last time you received a real paper message in your 'real' inbox at work? Chances are you may not be able to come up with a date. This is what makes a handwritten note important. They give pause because they are seen so rarely. Here are some key questions to consider.

What's it Gonna Cost?

- **Nothing You Can't Afford** – Handwritten notes require extra time to compose a thoughtful message and check your own grammar and spelling. These notes will also require a small investment in stamps, notecards, or stationery.

What Will You Get Out of it?

- **Benefits That Can't Be Denied** – You send a loud and clear message to the recipient. You are taking the time to convey appreciation or thanks in a more meaningful way than typical electronic communication.

What Are Some Occasions to Use a Handwritten Note?

- Acknowledging hard work
- Following up a meeting or conversation of importance
- Recognizing accomplishments
- Recognizing service anniversaries
- Expressing thanks, gratitude, or appreciation
- Celebrating birthdays
- Offering best wishes

In today's workplace, technology is a wonderful thing. It's a tool that improves processes and solves problems. It also creates opportunities for more time to accomplish the tasks that will help us to be successful. But don't forget to take a little of that 'saved time' and invest it in an old fashioned practice that will create a lasting impression on your colleagues.

REFERENCES

Toulmin, Stephen. The Uses of Argument. Cambridge University Press. New York, 1958.

In section three of this guide, '*The Business of Persuasion: The Toulmin Model and Persuasive Business Writing*, I apply the Toulmin Model to business writing. I focus on Stephen Toulmin's chapter three, '*The Layouts of Argument*' found in his book, The Uses of Argument. Within this chapter, Toulmin lays out a six part model as a framework for creating logic based arguments. Throughout this guide, I reference the elements of this framework and refer to them as the Toulmin Model in various chapters as a means to creating persuasive business documents.